CU00659734

UNSOCIAL MEDIA

Breaking Free from the Shackles of Social Media

by

CALVIN ROBBINS

Copyright © 2022 Calvin Robbins

All rights reserved.

No part of this publication may be reproduced, distributed or transmitted in any form or by any means, including photocopying, recording or other electronic or mechanical methods, without the prior written permission of the publisher, except in the case of brief quotations, reviews and other noncommercial uses permitted by copyright law.

Contents

About the author www.calvinrobbins.co.uk

Introduction

Social media has been majorly influential in modern society, positively and negatively. It gives people a way to stay connected, allows us to share fun, intriguing, and useful information in real-time, and also helps organisations attract clients.

So, while the bright side is that anyone can share anything – the dark side is: *anyone can share anything*. Of course, what we're referring to here is material that may not be true. Now and again, genuine mischief is made when individuals spread inflammatory, unconfirmed, or outright bogus data to confirm their biases. The 2016 US presidential election proved to be great evidence of this issue.

The Rise of Fake News Sites

Social media platforms have made it stupendously simple to spread ideas and data to a vast number of people in a short amount of time. On Facebook and Twitter in particular, users don't frequently fact check what is presented to them. A plethora of information is spread through videos, images, and infographics – even when the information is not founded on factual data. That means much of the images and videos on these platforms are made to be entertaining, charming, or crazy – as this is what drives engagement. Even connections to genuine articles can be deceiving – as many people who see sensational headlines never read the entire article.

Huffington Post recently distributed an intriguing examination featuring this precise issue. In the article "Bernie Sanders Could Replace President Trump With Little-Known Loophole", Matt Masur outlined the issue of individuals sharing articles that they didn't fact check or even read. In the subsequent section, Masur uncovered that many individuals shared articles without perusing them first.

Most phoney reports don't disclose that they are fake. In fact, there are even a few cases of what may be called *counterfeit* or parody news sites. The most popular of these is "The Onion", which is notorious for its satirical, sensational, and sarcastic headlines. As more humorous news sites crop up, it is becoming more challenging to recount whether a story is genuine or counterfeit. Of course, this goes hand in hand with the strange times that we live in, because sometimes even the most discerning people find it impossible to tell fact from fiction.

Many sites peddle this type of misleading content. They need users to tap on the articles to get clicks so they can sell additional "marketing". Other sites are those that are biased with what news they want to promote, whether they're left-wing right-wing or have a different agenda.

A teacher named Melissa Zimdars recently distributed a disputable rundown of fake news. This rundown refers to a few classifications of fake news sites that are regularly connected to Facebook. Any such list will undoubtedly be outdated, as new questionable news sites are continually being created. Zimdars' rundown has just gone under analysis for being one-sided against preservationists.

Regardless, the reality remains that there are currently several phoney news sites circulating bogus data all over the web.

The Harmful Impact of Fake News

Fake data is not a fake problem. In fact, this kind of bogus material has real world outcomes. Nowhere is this more obvious than in American politics. During the last political race, there was a story that attached Hillary Clinton to paedophilia and an illegal exploitation ring, which was widely shared on Facebook. Following an investigation, it turned out that this began with a solitary unverified post on a private group, before being reposted on many sites.

Social media stories, whether valid or not, have the potential to become a web sensation. The more unbelievable and newsworthy something is, the more certain it is that many individuals will share it. During the heat of a political race, supporters are inclined to share whatever makes their up-and-comer look like a winner, or whatever is most damaging to the opposition. This fact alone can create an echo chamber of bogus content. The worst part is that regardless of whether or not the claims are true, the damage in most cases has already been done.

It's no longer a stretch to claim that counterfeit reports influenced the result of the political decision. The Washington Post recently published a meeting with Paul Horner, somebody who confessed to composing many phoney reports about the political decision that were broadly distributed by Trump allies.

Instructions to Guard against Social Media Misinformation

It's the far-reaching potential of fake stories that causes real damage to social media. If you're an individual or business offering loads of information, maybe with the guide of social media programming, you need to be extra cautious. It takes only a moment or two to confirm whether something you see on social media is real. The general rule to follow is this: if you've never known about it, Google it and check whether it's true or not. If you don't have that much time, it's best to disregard it, especially if it resembles something that could be parody, misleading content, or publicity. By not sharing defective material, you're assisting with eliminating fake news from the internet.

Facebook CEO, Mark Zuckerberg, recently declared designs to get serious about fake news. Google has communicated similar expectations. It is not yet clear how powerful these proposals will be, given the size of social media today – where it can almost seem unrealistic to attempt to eradicate bogus data. At the end of the day, rather than point fingers and play the blame game, it's up to social media clients to do their due diligence and filter what they read, accept, and share.

Understanding the Impacts of Social Media: Pros and Cons

The landscape of social media has evolved tenfold in a relatively short period of time. This level of change has been unprecedented and we're now living among generations of people who have never known a world without it.

And it shows no signs of stopping any time soon. Technological innovation means that all over the world, most people have access to phones and, therefore social media. Now, this digital reality exists in everyone's pockets, and there's no cost for membership so everyone is on an even playing field.

What is the actual effect of Social Media?

Why People Share Information?

A captivating report by the New York Times Consumer Insight Group uncovered the main reasons people share data on social media. What did they find? Reasons included the following: A craving to reveal significant and engaging substance to other people; to characterise themselves; to develop and sustain connections, and to spread the news about brands and causes they like or support.

These variables have made social media advance from being just a convenient method for staying in contact with loved ones to being used in manners that affect society.

Effect of Social Media

1. The Impact of Social Media on Politics

According to Pew Research, 62% of people get their news reports from social media, with 18% doing so *all the time.*

In fact, in contrast with other media, social media's impact on political missions is majorly significant. These informal communities of people online play a significant part in constituent governmental issues — first seen in the last fruitless office of Howard Dean in 2003 and afterwards in the first African-American president's appointment in 2008.

This goes so far that the New York Times reported "The appointment of Donald J. Trump is maybe the starkest representation yet that over the earth, interpersonal organisations are serving to, on a fundamental level, rework human culture." This means that because social media allows individuals to speak with each other freely, shockingly persuasive social associations are being made in the most unlikely places.

2. The Impact of Social Media on Society

It's interesting that around a fourth of the total populace is currently on Facebook. In the USA, almost 80% of all web clients use this platform. Since informal communities feed off associations among individuals, they become even more impressive as they continue to develop.

Due to the nature of the internet, which is almost like the representation of the collective subconscious, every individual can find like minds, no matter how unique their views are. Humans are social creatures, and we crave a sense of belonging and familiarity. So, when like-minded people discover each other through social media, they get things done — make images, distributions, and create whole online universes that reinforce their perspective and afterwards, break into the standard.

Without social media, moral, social-ecological, and political ills would have negligible permeability into wider society. Now, we have access to a whole host of 'dirty laundry' almost instantly – allowing us to see what's truly going on behind the scenes.

On the flip side? Social media is gradually replacing genuine activism with 'slacktivism.'

Slacktivism is the practice of supporting a political or social cause through social media or online petitions, which naturally involves very little effort or commitment. Simply retweeting, sharing and liking posts then replaces actual protests.

So, while social media activism brings expanded mindfulness about cultural issues, there are still questions about whether this mindfulness actually translates to genuine change, or if – like most things on social media – it's just a fabricated illusion.

This is a distinctly human response, and when individuals are given alternatives that absolve them from the duty to act – they'll take the path of least resistance. This idea is backed by a recent report from the University of British Columbia's Sauder School of Business, which found that when individuals are given the alternative of 'enjoying' a social cause, they prefer this over sacrificing time and cash. Then again, when individuals are permitted to support in private, they tend to give significant help where money commitments are concerned.

3. The Impact of Social Media on Commerce

Since social media is now part of the fabric of our everyday reality, this almost implies that it is strange to discover groups of like-minded people offline than online. Organisations know this, and they see the significance of using social media to interact with clients for the purpose of generating income.

Organisations use social media to produce bits of knowledge, invigorate requests, and focus on item contributions. This is significant for the industry of e-commerce and general online business.

It has been suggested that such connections in the work environment can reinforce information sharing. That's because social advancements in the work environment eliminate limits and can raise collaboration to cultivate a work culture of more gifted and educated employees.

The other side: Low number of social 'shares' or likes means that businesses might not be taken as seriously as they should be.

Curiously, even though the usage of social sharing has become the standard in business, a few organisations have chosen to contradict some shared norms and eliminate this aspect of social media from their sites.

A contextual investigation of Taloon.com, a social business retailer from Finland, discovered that transformations rose by 11.9% when they eliminated share catches from their item pages.

These outcomes feature the double-edged nature of the effect of social media. When items draw in a lot of offers, they can fortify deals. This is what Dr Paul Marsden, clinician, and writer of 'The Social Commerce Handbook,' alluded to as 'social verification.'

4. The Impact of Social Media on the World of Work

Social media has profoundly affected enlistment and recruiting, so much so that 19% of recruiting officers settle on their employing choices using data found on social media. As showed by CareerBuilder's 2016 social media enrolment overview, 60% of bosses use informal communication sites to vet work applicants.

Professional, informal organisations, like LinkedIn, are significant social media platforms for anybody hoping to dwell in their calling. They permit individuals to make and market an individual brand.

5. The Impact of Social Media on Training and Development

Educators and those who sell "learning" are doing tremendously on social media.

A 2013 study by Pearson Learning Solutions revealed a significant increase in social media use for learning. A large portion of the teachers who were met concurred that social sharing supports connection, creating a space that encourages learning.

Online journals, wikis, LinkedIn, Twitter, Facebook, and webcasts are now traditional instruments for learning in many instructive establishments. Social media has added to the expansion in significant distance social learning.

Regardless of the lack of protection in an online environment, and a few cases of cheating among significant distance students – this has not deflected social platforms from being used in training.

6. *The Challenges of Social Media*

Social media has been accused of advancing social ills, for example:

Cyberbullying:

Young people, especially adolescents, have an intrinsic need to fit in, to be well known, and to outdo others. This cycle was tested long before the advent of social media. But now, digital spaces like Facebook, Twitter, Snapchat, and Instagram, with the general mish-mash, mean that young people are being exposed to more than they normally would, and are growing up too fast in an online world.

Michael Hamm, an analyst from the University of Alberta, led an examination that showed social media enables bullying. In his analyses, 23% of adolescent social media users reported being picked on, and 15% said they'd bullied somebody on social media. Adolescents can abuse social media platforms to spread bits of gossip, share videos and images intended for bullying, and coerce others.

Absence of Privacy:

Stalking, fraud, individual assaults, and data abuse represent just one portion of the dangers faced by social media clients. More often than not, the clients themselves are also at fault, as they wind up sharing details that should not be in the public eye. This merging of the public and private is a common occurrence on social media. As previously mentioned, the internet functions almost like the collective unconscious – so when people share intimate details online, it feels different than standing on a soap box and airing out their secrets.

Nobody would do the latter, but plenty of people share intimate details online every single day.

Tragically, when the private information is erased, it's already past the point of no return and can continue to haunt an individual's life even years after.

7. The Impact of Social Media on Relationships

One effect of social media is it compels individuals to shape and appreciate fake or pretentious bonds over genuine friendships. The term 'friend' as used on social media comes up short on the closeness associated with traditional relationships, where individuals know one another deeply, need to converse with one another, and have a personal bond.

The Bottom Line

It's been said that data is power. Without a method for disseminating data, individuals can't tackle its sheer force. One major effect of social media today is the appropriation of data. Platforms, for example, Facebook,

LinkedIn, Twitter, and others, have made it conceivable to obtain significant data in just a flash.

Exploration directed by parse.ly shows that the lifespan of a story posted on the web is 2.6 days, contrasted with 3.2 days when a story is shared on social media. That is a distinction of 23%, which is enormous when you consider that billions of individuals use the web daily.

This implies that the more drawn out the data is available for use, the more conversation it creates, and the more prominent social media is.

While the world would be a much quieter spot without social media, it's caused as much good as it has harm. Indeed, the positive effect of social media is cosmic.

At the end of the day, sharing is tied in with getting individuals to see and react to content. The requirement for data exists, it's consistently helpful for any association to use social media to continue providing news and updates.

CHAPTER ONE

Effects Of Social Media On Mental Health

Most young people today use social media, on a daily basis. Since 45% of teenagers detailing that they are online "continually," and another 44% say they are online at least a few times a day, the effect of social media on the young mind is being called into question.

What are the main social media platforms, and how are they used?

Over 40% of young ladies and over 20% of young adult men report using social media for at least 3 hours per day. The most well-known social media platforms are

Snapchat, Instagram, Facebook, YouTube, TikTok, and Twitter.

Snapchat permits its users to share photographs that vanish once they have been opened, just as "stories" disappear following 24 hours. These "accounts" enable users to share their encounters with all their supporters through videos or pictures.

Instagram has a choice for users to share "stories" for 24 hours too, but it also allows sharing pictures or videos that stay on a user's profile. Unless somebody sets their Instagram account to "private," anybody can look at the posted photographs and videos. Many people use Instagram for photograph blogging, posting videos from excursions or everyday life, and sharing their interests in art, cooking, and different exercises. In recent years, Instagram has been taken over by "influencer" culture – those with a large following tend to advertise a certain lifestyle to their followers.

Facebook lets its users share photographs, videos, and articles and data about their lives, just as talking with friends.

YouTube permits users to share unique videos, such as music, cooking, make-up tutorials and video blogs (online video journals) or anything else you can imagine.

Twitter allows its users to share their thoughts as an individual update in 280 characters or less.

These social media platforms are used to speak with friends and are famous sources of news and for following what celebrities and famous people post.

The advantages of social media

In a 2018 overview, 31% of teenagers accepted that social media had a specific effect on their life. That's because social media is a great place for young people to foster friendships. It provides teenagers with a structured network and enables them to stay in contact with friends who don't live close by, and it can also help those who are socially awkward or underdeveloped.

Is social media associated with emotional wellness issues?

Despite all the talk of social media allowing individuals to connect with others, it also has the potential to bring out the dark side in people. Practically 25% of young people accept that social media has a generally negative impact.

With 13% of long-term users developing depression and 32% developing anxiety, psychological sickness is a worrying symptom of social media use. This is even more worrying with the fact that 25% of long-term users report having some psychological disorder. Among girls, a more melancholic attitude is not unheard of. This has risen to such an extent that some scientists believe the increase in dysfunctional behaviour is associated with the increase in social media use among young people.

But the question remains, how does social media hurt psychological wellness? Many of these investigations show that time spent on social media platforms is associated with depression and anxiety, but that doesn't imply that social media causes these issues, right? The answer is inconclusive, but it may surprise you. Does using social media prompt depression and anxiety, or do depressed and anxious individuals use social media more than their friends? Well, now there is research to back up this claim. For instance, in one examination from 2020, individuals who deactivated their Facebook for a month revealed lower levels of depression and anxiety, with an added increase in joy and life fulfilment.

One common issue that has been accepted as a good answer for why social media leads to negative mental health, is that of disturbed sleep, and poor sleep regulation can lead to depression and anxiety. Social media use around evening time upsets sleep, in various manners: people stay awake until late on the web, the blue light from the screen can disturb the circadian rhythm, and many individuals wake up at night to check or react to messages. Many young people report that they use social media around evening time, and it affects their sleep. There is an unspoken stress that if they don't use their phone around evening time, it will lead to passing up social opportunities. This is also known as FOMO (fear of missing out). What's more? Teenagers report that their friends expect them to be accessible all evening. There is also the pressure to respond to messages quickly.

Social media tends to compound sentiments of FOMO, for instance, if somebody sees posts about a gathering that they were not welcomed to. Young people are mostly defenceless against the adverse effects of social media, because social connectedness is significant for their turn of events.

Depression and anxiety are not the only psychological wellness issues related to social media use. For teens, it also affects their self-esteem, whether male or female. For example, staring at a stream of aesthetically attractive people will inevitably lead to "body observation," checking one's own body and getting critical about it. Individuals who regularly scrutinize their bodies report feeling more disgrace about their bodies. On Instagram in particular – the platform designed for posting images – there is a whole host of "fitspiration" accounts posting about clean eating regimens and exercise, as well as accounts of those who have had a myriad of cosmetic surgery procedures. What this means is that whether "natural" or surgical bodies are being promoted, individuals feel a greater need to channel or photoshop their posts on Instagram to eliminate imperfections. Individuals compare themselves with these beliefs or these altered pictures and feel like they don't have the right stuff. This can cause low self-esteem.

Social media is also a playground for cyberbullying. In fact, 72% of adolescents stated that they had been bullied online at some point. Due to the nature of how cyberbullying occurs, its victims of cyberbullying can't move away from it – it remains on the web, and occurs far beyond the sight of those who can stop it, like educators and guardians.

What can guardians do?

Since kids in particular are vulnerable to peer pressure, social media sites can be a hazardous spot to "hang out." The Children's Online Privacy Protection Act disallows sites from gathering data on people younger than 13 without parental authorisation. However, since the age depends on self-report, kids younger than 13 can lie about their age and open records. The New York Board of Education has an asset manual to help kids above 13 years old use the web more securely and soundly.

Let's face it, many parents or guardians have absolutely no idea how social media works or what it even entails – and with their busy schedules, this leaves multiple children alone on the web, which can prompt issues. Parental management is as important online as it is offline when it comes to safeguarding children. There are various tools to help show guardians' social media sites and how they work. Associate safely has created "parent guides" for understanding distinctive social media platforms.

Common Sense Media has a rundown of "warnings" to watch out for when your kids are using different social media platforms – and some just might surprise you.

Parents and guardians should check in routinely with their children to guarantee that their online conduct is age-appropriate and suitable. Observing your child on social media might seem like a good option, but the truth is – they will find a way around it. Instead of giving your children an excuse to be sneaky, it's much better to talk to them about social media use early and construct a relationship of trust. This way, children and adolescents will be much more likely to tell you when there is an issue.

One thing you can do is check in with your kids and let them know it is safe to come to you if they are being cyberbullied. Safe Teens has built up a site with data about cyberbullying. You can browse and talk about this website with your kids.

Another significant discussion to have with your kids is about how social media can influence their emotions. As noted in this book, many social media users get depressed or have low self-esteem when they compare themselves with others and feeling like they don't have the right 'stuff' – whether that's material gains or their physical body. It is essential to remind your kids that social media does not represent reality.

Tips for monitoring social media use

- Pick a period around evening time after which you won't check your phone, and if possible, charge your phone in another room while you rest.

- Use a morning timer instead of depending on your phone as a caution to keep you from using your phone the moment you wake up.

- Choose one day a week when you take a break from social media and spotlight different things.

- Turn off your notifications for a couple of hours every day (which you can bit by bit expand); put your phone on "Plane" mode or "Don't Disturb."

- Set limits or just certain occasions when you can check your notices.

- Take a break from applications that you notice add to unfortunate self-perception. Instead, you can add applications intended to help you rest comfortable thinking about yourself, such as reflection applications.

- Use applications that block specific apps and inform you about your usage. This will help expand your consciousness of the amount you are drawing in with social media and help you zero in on different exercises.

- Start the habit of putting your phone next to the door when you get back home — doing it with a friend, accomplice, or relative can help you remain inspired and responsible! Arrange with a gathering of friends to invest more energy hanging out face to face and less time cooperating through social media.

- Consider placing your phone in grayscale. This makes your phone less alluring to look at. With the vivid applications and warnings changed to dark, they might be easier to ignore.

The role social media plays in emotional wellbeing.

As humans, we're social animals. We need friendship and familiarity as much as we need air to breathe, and the quality of our associations hugely affects our emotional wellbeing. Strong bonds with others can ease pressure, anxiety and misery, and support healthy self-esteem. On the other side, lacking solid social associations can present a genuine danger to your psychological wellbeing – from low self-esteem to loneliness.

In this day and age, many of us depend on social media platforms, such as Facebook, Twitter, Snapchat, YouTube, TikTok and Instagram, to keep up with friends and acquaintances. While this may have its advantages, social media can never be a substitution for real human contact. We didn't evolve to have our needs met by digital screens – we evolved requiring face-to-face contact. Ironically, for an innovation intended to unite individuals, expending an excessive amount of energy on social media platforms can cause people to feel lonelier and more confined—compounding psychological wellbeing issues, such as depression and anxiety.

The positive face of social media

Sure, virtual communication on social media can never live up to the advantages of having personal contact, but despite the doom and gloom, there are many positive aspects to using social media too.

Social media empowers you to:

- Communicate and stay connected with loved ones around the globe.

- Find new friends and networks; network with others who share similar interests or aspirations.

- Join or advance practical purposes; create awareness for significant matters.

- Seek or offer enthusiastic help during hard times.

- Foster indispensable social connections if you live in a distant zone, for instance, or have restricted freedom, social anxiety, or are essential for a minimised gathering.

- Find an outlet for your creativity and self-articulation.

- Discover (with care) wellsprings of essential data and learning.

The negative parts of social media

Dissatisfaction with your life or appearance is among the main side effects of too much social media use. Regardless of whether you realise that pictures on social media are manipulated, fabricated or illusory – they can cause you to feel unhappy about what you look like or even what's happening in your own life. In a broad sense, people tend to showcase their life's highlight reel, not the drudgery of their everyday routines. Yet, even this common knowledge doesn't seem to decrease those sentiments of jealousy and disappointment when you're flicking through a friend's digitally embellished photographs of their tropical seashore event or finding out about their energising new promotion at work.

FOMO (the fear of missing out) has been around far longer than social media – it's almost hardwired into our human makeup. But that doesn't mean social media can't make this feeling worse, it happens to do so quite often. The possibility that you're passing up specific things and missing out can affect your confidence, trigger uneasiness, and fuel even more social media use. FOMO is the single force propelling you to constantly refresh, or enthusiastically react to every single alarm or notification — whether you're driving, passing up rest around evening time, or choosing social media communication over genuine connections.

If there's one thing at the core of this social media FOMO frenzy, it's this: *isolation*. One study at the University of Pennsylvania found that although a high usage of Facebook, Snapchat, and Instagram increased depressive symptoms, social media use also made people feel less lonely and segregated when used sensibly.

But the fact remains, if people substitute human connection with social media connections, the higher the risk of depression and anxiety. We need real, tangible human contact in order to have our basic emotional needs met – and the blue glow of a digital screen simply cannot replace that.

Sharing endless selfies or your most profound achievements to accumulate validation in the form of likes, shares and comments can make you feel good for the moment – but on the other hand, it can also make you reliant on others' approval, and make you critical of how you present yourself.

What's driving your social media use?

Nowadays, there's no real distinction between the online and offline world. While this makes it helpful to stay in contact, it implies that social media is consistently 'open'. This nonstop, hyper network can trigger control issues, until you're held captive by your phone. After all, your possessions will possess you if you're not careful.

The endless loop of undesirable social media use

Unreasonable social media use can create a negative, self-propagating cycle:

1. When you feel discouraged, dissatisfied, or restless, you use social media more regularly—as an approach to ease fatigue or to feel associated with others.

2. Using social media expands FOMO and sentiments of distress, disappointment, and detachment.

3. These sentiments adversely influence your temperament and side effects of sadness, anxiety, and stress.

4. These compounding side effects cause you to use social media more, and the cycle continues.

Signs that social media is affecting your emotional wellbeing:

Everybody is unique. There is no standard measure of time spent on social media, how often you refresh, or the number of posts that make you feel bad about yourself. It's different for everyone.

For instance, your social media use might be dangerous if it makes you disregard your everyday life and responsibilities, distracts you from work or school or leaves you feeling anxious, angry, or discouraged. If you begin to feel like you want to escape from your life into the clutches of your phone, it might be time to re-evaluate the importance social media has over your own life.

But if there's one thing to remember, it's this: even if you have thousands of followers leaving comments on your social media activities – at the end of the day, you are alone smiling at a screen. Those followers are not physically with you, they are all suspended in their own technological world-of-one just like you are with your phone. They don't communicate as real people, but rather through flat avatars. So it's important for you to determine how much is too much.

Pointers that social media might be negatively influencing your psychological wellbeing include:

You are investing more energy on social media than with your real-life friends.

Using social media has become a substitute for a ton of your disconnected social collaboration. Regardless of whether you're out with friends, you always want to check social media because you feel that others might be having a better time than you, or that you might be missing out on something else.

You are comparing yourself to others on social media.

You have low confidence or negative self-esteem. You may even have an eating disorder creep up on you without realising it.

You deal with cyberbullying.

Or you stress that you have no power over the things individuals post about you.

You are distracted at school or work.

You crave the dopamine hit of a notification, so you make posts, comments and other content.

You don't give yourself any time for self-reflection.

Each extra second is filled by social media, leaving you very little time for your own development.

You take part in dangerous behaviour for positive responses on social media.

You play risky tricks, post humiliating material, cyberbully others, or access your phone while driving or in other dangerous circumstances.

You experience sleep issues.

Do you check social media last thing at night or first thing in the morning? The light from phones and different gadgets can disturb your rest, seriously affecting your psychological wellbeing.

You feel that your depression and anxiety is getting worse. As opposed to lifting your mood and mindset, you feel more restless, discouraged, or distressed after using social media.

Changing social media use to improve emotional wellbeing:

Stage 1: Reduce time on the web

This one seems like a no brainer, but it's much easier said than done. A 2018 University of Pennsylvania study found that reducing social media use to just 30 minutes daily brought about a significant decrease in anxiety, gloom, depression, sleep disorders, and FOMO. A similar report inferred that merely being more aware of what you consume on social media use can benefit your mindset and core interest.

While 30 minutes daily may not be a sensible aim for most of us who spend hours scrolling, we can still gain significant advantages by reducing the time we spend on social media. The accompanying tips can help:

1. Use an application to monitor how much time you spend on social media every day. At that point, set an aim for the amount you need to decrease it by.

2. Turn off your phone at specific times, for example, when you're driving, with friends, at the gym, eating, or playing with your children. Try not to take your phone with you to the restroom.

3. Don't carry your phone or tablet to bed. Turn gadgets off and leave them in another room to charge.

4. Disable notifications. It's difficult to ignore the consistent humming, signalling, and dinging of your phone, making you aware of new messages. Disabling notifications can assist you with recovering control of your time and core interest.

5. Limit checks if you urgently check your phone at regular intervals; wean yourself off by restricting your checks to once an hour and then gradually decrease this. Some applications can consequently limit when you're ready to get to your phone.

6. Try moving social media applications from your phone to your tablet or PC. If this seems like too much, eliminate each app to perceive the amount you genuinely miss it.

Stage 2: Change your core interest

What a lot of people don't realise is that social media has become a habitual part of their daily routine, and old habits die hard. In fact, most of us access social media without really thinking – it's just a reflex action. However, by zeroing in on your inspiration for checking your socials, you not only diminish the time you spend on them, you also improve your experience and maintain a strategic distance from a significant number of the negative angles.

So, next time you go to get to social media, put everything on hold, and explain your *why*.

Is it true that you are using social media as a substitute for reality? Is there a more helpful substitute for your social media use? In case you're desperate for an escape, for instance, invite a friend out for an espresso. Were you feeling discouraged? Go for a stroll or go to the gym. Exhausted? Take up another hobby. Social media might be fast and helpful, but there's a whole world out there to explore beyond the confines of your screen.

Does social media leave you feeling lacking or frustrated about your life? You can counter FOMO by practising gratitude. And it's pretty easy: Make a list of the good in your life and read it back when you feel you're passing up something better. Also, recall: nobody's life is ever as impeccable as it appears on social media. We all suffer anguish, self-uncertainty, and dissatisfaction, regardless of whether we decide not to share it on the web.

Stage 3: Spend additional time with friends

We need to have a personal connection with others. At its best, social media is an incredible instrument for encouraging genuine relationships. But if you're spending more time with virtual friends than real-life friends – consider why this is. Is it because you feel you cannot connect to the people around you? Or is it because you need to work on building genuine relationships.

Set aside time every week to connect with loved ones. Attempt to make it a regular party where you keep your phones off. Once you build a habit, it will be hard to break.

You can also connect with an old friend (or an online friend) and plan a get-together. If you both have busy lives, offer to get things done or practice together.

Join a club. Discover a side interest, hobby, or wellness movement you appreciate and join a group of like-minded people that meet consistently. At the end of the day, the opposite of depression is movement. If you are feeling low on energy and depressed, joining a club that revolves around movement is a great idea to stimulate those happy hormones and keep you hopeful. It can be dancing, pilates, a spin class or anything else you might like. Explore your options, you'll be surprised how many accessible clubs there are.

Try not to let social awkwardness disrupt your flow. Regardless of whether you're modest or just a little shy, there are methods to build confidence and build connections!

Suppose you don't feel that you have anybody to invest energy with, try to reach out to people and be friendly. You'd be surprised just how many other people feel the same way, so be the one to break the ice. Invite a colleague out for lunch or ask a neighbour or schoolmate to go along with you for an espresso.

Collaborate with outsiders. Turn upward from your screen and associate with individuals you encounter on an open vehicle, café, or markets. Smiling or making proper acquaintance will improve how you feel—and no one can tell where it might lead.

Stage 4: Express appreciation

Being grateful for the essential things throughout your life can eliminate the hatred, hostility, and discontent now and again created by social media. Chances are, if you have a roof over your head, food in your belly and no immediate threats to your livelihood – you are richer than most people in the world.

Set aside effort for reflection. Take a stab at keeping an appreciation diary or using an appreciation app. Monitor all the incredible recollections and encouraging points throughout your life—like things and individuals you'd miss if they were gone from your life. In case you're more inclined to venting or negative posts, you can even offer your thanks on social media—even though you may profit more from the private reflection that isn't dependent on others.

Practice care. Rather than being wholly occupied with the present, you're centred around the "if only's" that keep you from having a daily existence that coordinates those you see on social media. By practising care, you can figure out how to live, decrease FOMO's effect, and improve your general mental prosperity.

Have you ever considered volunteering? Human beings are hard-wired to look for the social association, we're hard-wired to provide for other people. Helping others will not just help them, it is also critical for you; it causes you to feel more joyful and more thankful – as well as giving you a sense of purpose and accomplishment.

Helping a kid or teenager with unfortunate social media use

Adolescence is a tender and tricky transitional time – it's when children become pre-adults, and crave independence and a sense of identity. Social media can make this time worse, by making impressionable teens feel inadequate, and if you're a parent, you might be tempted to confiscate their gadgets. But rather than being an overprotective parent, which will in fact make your teens want to rebel – you should have a lengthy chat with them about social media and its effects. Not only will it make them more likely to come to you when they need help, it also teaches them about informed decision making.

Monitor and limit your teen's social media use, rather than outright banning them. The more you think about how your kid is communicating on social media, the better you'll have the option to address any issues. Parental control applications can help limit your child's use or confine their phone usage to specific times.

Also, you can change security settings on the various platforms to restrict their exposure to inappropriate content and predatory behaviour.

Uphold "social media" breaks. For instance, you could boycott social media until your child has finished their schoolwork at night, not permit phones during dinner or in their room, and plan family exercises that boycott phones or different gadgets. To prevent sleep disorders, make sure that phones are turned off one hour before bed.

Show your children how social media isn't an exact impression of individuals' lives. You can use your own social media experience to guide them too, after all, you're reading this book for a reason. Social media followers, likes and comments are like having monopoly money in real life. Sure, it's fun during the game – but the game has to end at some point.

You can also move your child away from social media by urging them to seek their own interests, like physical exercise or activities that include teamwork. Activity is incredible for alleviating anxiety and stress, boosting confidence, and improving mindset—and is something you can do as a family. The more your kid is connected to real life and real results, the less their self-esteem will be subject to the number of friends, likes, or offers they have on social media.

CHAPTER TWO

Unhealthy Smartphone Addiction

What is smartphone addiction?

While a phone, tablet, or PC can be an enormously useful possession, *it can also possess you*. If you invest more energy in social media or messing around than you do interacting with individuals in your daily life, or you can't prevent yourself from consistently checking messages, or applications—even when it has adverse outcomes in your life—it might be an ideal opportunity to evaluate your use of social media.

This kind of fixation is informally known as "nomophobia" (fear of being without a phone) and is frequently energised by an Internet abuse issue or Internet compulsion issue. It's rarely the phone or tablet itself that makes the impulse, yet instead the games, apps, and online universes it exposes us to.

Phone habit can envelop an assortment of motor control issues, including:

> **Virtual connections:** Dependence on interpersonal communication, dating applications, messaging, and informing can stretch out where virtual, online friends become more significant than genuine relationships. We've all observed the couples sitting together in a café, ignoring one another, and focusing on their phones. While the Internet can be an incredible spot to meet new individuals, reconnect with old friends, or even begin sentimental connections, online connections are not reliable substitutes for genuine connections. While your online friends may seem more enticing – you have ot remember that the friendship is not subject to the same trials and tribulations that your real-life friendships go through. Social media is a sanitised and sterilised world.

Data over-burden: Habitual web surfing, watching videos, messing around, or checking news channels can mess with your focus at work or school and distract you for quite a long time. Impulsive use of the Internet and phone applications can make you disregard different parts of your life, without you realising, from proper connections to interests and social interests.

Cybersex fixation: Let's not beat around the bush, the internet exposes young developing brains to a whole world of completely inappropriate and damaging content. Porn is freely available, without any regulation. Like a drug, the dopamine produced from watching porn wanes over time, prompting people to consume pornographic content that is even more "hardcore" just to feel the same pleasure. This becomes an addiction that messes with your mental health and even bleeds into your real-life relationships. It is inherently damaging no matter how much people defend it. Plus, excessive use of dating apps that encourage casual sex can make it harder to grow long-term personal connections or harm a current relationship. Relationships become a commodity, and it can feel like you're always "shopping" for the next best one.

For example, online impulses, like gaming, betting, stock exchanging, social shopping, or sites like eBay, can cause spending addictions that cripple your budget or worse, incur debt. While betting addiction has existed since the dawn of time, the accessibility of Internet betting has made this even more accessible. Impulsive stock exchanging can be harmful, especially when people lack knowledge of how to invest. eBay addicts may wake up at odd hours to be online for the last minutes of a closeout. You may buy things you don't really need and can't manage the cost of, just to experience the high of winning an auction.

Circumstances and results of phone and Internet dependence

While you can only use your PC in one place, phones and tablets' mean we can stay connected no matter where we are – as long as there's WiFi or phone data.

This is not a small societal change; its effects have been seismic! We're living in a cultural shift, evidenced by many studies. Perhaps the most notable study on the effects of social media is this one from the UK.

The study found that individuals who invest a great deal of energy on social media demonstrate dark triad traits, such as elevated narcissism. Snapping unending selfies, posting every one of your contemplations or insights concerning your life can create undesirable narcissism, separating you from genuine connections and making it harder to adapt to pressure.

This results in a culture of narcissism and individualism – making us more self-absorbed and selfish.

If you use your phone as a "familiar object" to reduce feelings of unease, depression, or social awkwardness, you're succumbing to avoidant behaviours rather than facing your challenges and building resilience. Gazing at your phone will deny you the up close and personal collaborations that can help you become familiar with other people, ease anxiety, and lift your disposition. The cure you're deciding for your uneasiness (drawing in with your phone) is exacerbating your anxiety!

Phone or Internet compulsion can also adversely affect your life by:

One scientist found that the simple presence of a phone in a workplace will put employees on edge and cause them to perform inadequately.

The fact is, using a phone for work means that work seeps into your home and personal life. You feel like you need to stay on top of whatever comes next in work, and this need to respond to emails can add to higher feelings of anxiety and even burnout. To prevent this, you need a good work-life balance, and this can't be achieved if you're always checking your phone for work updates even when you're off the clock.

The consistent stream of messages and data from a phone can overpower your mind and make it challenging to focus for more than a couple of minutes without feeling constrained to proceed onward to something different. No matter how many hours you have in your day, each of us has a limited cognitive capacity –once you're mentally tired, it's not possible to keep going

You are upsetting your rest. The importance of quality rest cannot be overstated. It can affect your memory, diminish your intellectual and learning aptitudes and make you emotionally dysregulated.

Signs and side effects of phone addiction

Have you been discovering laundry piling up and little food in the house for dinner since you've been caught up with browsing, messaging, or playing computer games? Maybe you end up working late more frequently because you can't finish your work on time.

Is phone activity affecting the time you spend with your loved ones? Are you starting to feel like nobody in your "real" life—even your life partner—understands you like your online friends?

Are you covering your phone use? Do you sneak off to a peaceful spot to use your phone? Do you cover up your phone use or lie to your family about the amount of time you spend on the web? Do you get disturbed or irritable if your online time is intruded on?

Are you experiencing FOMO? Do you prefer not to feel unaware of present circumstances or believe you're passing up important news or data if you don't check your phone? Do you impulsively check social media because you're on edge that others are making some better memories or living a more exciting life than you?

The sentiment of fear, anxiety, or frenzy on the off chance you leave your phone at home, or the battery runs down. Or do you "feel" phantom vibrations—you think your phone has vibrated; but when you check, there are no new messages or updates?

Withdrawal side effects from phone enslavement

Typical warning signs of phone or Internet dependence may include:

- Restlessness
- Anger or crabbiness
- Difficulty concentrating
- Sleep disorders
- Craving your phone or another gadget
- Inability to be alone without phone

Self-improvement tips for phone addiction

There are various techniques you can take to get your phone and Internet use levelled out. While you can start many of these measures yourself, an addiction is challenging to beat all alone. Ask a friend to keep you accountable when you start!

To help you recognise your pain points, keep a log of when and how you use your phone for non-work or insignificant exercises. There are specific applications that can help with this, enabling you to monitor the time you spend on your phone. Are there hours of the day that you use your phone more? Are there different things you could be doing? The more you understand your phone use, the simpler it will be to recover control of your time.

Identify the triggers that make you go after your phone. Is it when you're lonely or exhausted? If you are battling with melancholy, stress, or anxiety, for instance, your excessive phone use may be an approach to self-soothe harmful mindsets. Instead, discover more helpful and more noble methods of dealing with your states of mind.

Understand the distinction between connecting face-to-face and on the web. Individuals are social animals. We're not meant to be disconnected or to depend on technology for human association. Interacting with someone else up close and personal—visually connecting, reacting to non-verbal communication—can cause you to feel quiet, safe, and comprehended, and immediately ease the pressure. Associating through content or email won't have a similar impact on your enthusiastic prosperity. Plus, online friends can't embrace you when an emergency hits, visit you when you're debilitated, or attend a local festive event with you.

Deconstruct your coping mechanisms. Maybe tweeting, messaging, or blogging is your method of adapting to pressure or outrage. Or then again, perhaps you have trouble identifying with others and think it's more straightforward to speak with individuals on the web. Addressing these areas of your personality will help you endure the anxieties and strains of day-to-day existence without depending on your phone.

Adjust your phone use, bit by bit

Don't quit cold turkey. Consider it more like starting a better eating routine. Just as you need to eat, you presumably still need to use your phone for work, school, or contact with friends. Your aim ought to be to scale back to a healthier level of consumption.

1. Set objectives for when you can use your phone. For instance, you may plan to use it for specific occasions of the day. You could reward yourself with an extra 30 mins on your phone once you've finished a task or completed an errand.

2. Turn off your phone at specific times, for example, when you're driving, in a gathering, at the gym, eating, or playing with your children. Try not to take your phone with you to the washroom.

3. Don't carry your phone or tablet to bed. The blue light transmitted by the screens can upset your sleep whenever used within two hours of sleep time. Turn gadgets off and leave them in another room to charge. Rather than using eBooks on your phone or tablet, get a book. You'll rest better and recollect a more significant amount of what you've read.

4. Replace your phone use with more practical exercises. If you are exhausted and sad, fighting the temptation to use your phone can be troublesome. Have an arrangement for different approaches to occupy the time, such as meditating, reading a book, or visiting friends.

5. Play the "phone stack" game. When you're eating, having drinks together, have everybody place their phones face down on the table. Even if the phones buzz, nobody must snatch their gadget. If somebody can't avoid checking their phone, that individual needs to pay the bill for everybody.

6. Remove social media applications from your phone so you have to check Facebook, Twitter, etc. from your PC. Also, remember that what you see on social media is seldom an accurate impression of their lives—individuals misrepresent the positive parts of their lives, and don't showcase their behind-the-scenes frustrations. Stop comparing yourself with these fabricated fantasies and boost your state of mind and feelings of self-esteem through gratitude.

7. Curb your fear of passing up a significant opportunity. Acknowledge that by restricting your phone use, you're probably going to pass up specific requests, breaking news, or new gossip. There is so much data accessible on the Internet, and it's practically impossible to keep up with everything. Tolerating this can be freeing and help break your dependence.

Remedy for phone and Internet addiction

If you need more help to not check your phone or Internet use, there are currently great treatment focuses that offer advanced detox projects to assist you with disengaging from social and digital media. Individual and group therapy can also give you a major lift in controlling your internet use.

Therapy has the added benefit of helping you deal with the social awkwardness, stress, anxiety, or depression— that might be powering your phone use.

There are groups online that you can join, like Internet Tech Addiction Anonymous (ITAA) and Online Gamers

Anonymous, that offer online help and physical meetings for those struggling with social media use. And don't feel any shame about sex addiction because Sex Addicts Anonymous can be a spot to attempt in case you're experiencing difficulty with cybersex dependence.

There is help out there, you just have to seek it out with the same gusto as you seek out social media.

Assisting a child or adolescent with phone addiction

Any parent who's attempted to drag a child or teen away from a phone or tablet realises how testing it is to isolate kids from social media, or social games and videos. With the younger generations, they are already born into a world where social media is a part of everyday reality. Not taking part, can feel like not being a part of society. It's harder for them, but not impossible to cut down on use.

Young people are impressionable and have a solid motivation to mirror those around them, so show them that life can be lived offline too! Try not to be a hypocrite if you find yourself using your social media too – as this sends out the wrong kind of message.

Make "phone-free" zones around the home. Confine the use of phones or tablets to a typical house zone where you can monitor them and give them a web curfew. Restrict phones from the dinner table and rooms, and demand they're turned off at a specific time.

Encourage different interests and social exercises. Move your child or teen away from screens by presenting other side interests and exercises, such as group activities, Scouts, and after-school clubs. Invest energy as a family unplugged.

Regularly check in with your child about how they are feeling Urgent phone use may indicate more urgent issues. Is your child having problems fitting in? Has there been a significant ongoing change, similar to a move or separation, causing pressure? Is your kid enduring different issues at school or at home?

Find support. Children and teens like to rebel against their caretakers; however, if they hear a similar thought from an alternate source, they might be more inclined to listen. Attempt to get a games mentor, specialist, or regarded family friend in on the action.

4 Ways You Can Add Value to Your Life by Valuing Your Time

Time is everything in this life. One of the most important things to consider is reaching your maximum potential and making the most out of your time, so you don't feel as though you wasted your life. We have limited time on this planet to do what we like to do because once it's gone, *it's gone*. No do-over, no time machine. Just the present moment.

#1 – Value Your Time by Getting Organised

This is irrefutably the initial step you must take when trying to take more control of your time. Ensure you're getting sorted out and seeing precisely how you're investing that energy. At that point, plan how you will use your time and energy later on. Start by recording how long your daily routine takes. At that point, make a list of how you need to invest your energy. Record your objectives and desires, drill down the things you love, and make day-by-day plans. You'll see how rapidly you gain more energy for doing the things you need to do. Consistency is key.

#2 – Value Your Time by Creating Time Accountability Relating to Others

Do you say yes to everything, and are you always ready to answer messages or Tweets immediately? This shows others that your time *is theirs*. You'll always be accessible and show that you're not doing anything for yourself. But by answering messages during particular hours of your day, you make your time considerably more elite and valuable.

This has various advantages, including investing more energy in doing what you love and making time spent with others more significant and beneficial.

#3 – Value Your Time by Committing Time to Your Health

Your wellbeing relies upon how much energy you need to spend on doing other purposeful things in your life and is the benchmark to foe what you're capable of accomplishing. This implies you have to ensure you're investing energy in ensuring your wellbeing is ideal.

#4 – Value Your Time by reflecting and Analysing

While it's acceptable to consider the future and plan, it's similar, if not more critical, to invest energy pondering your past. This isn't to say you should dwell on past mistakes or live in the past, but it's critical to think about how interesting you've been, and whether you could make even better achievements down the line. This is an extraordinary method to ensure you're investing your energy shrewdly and taking the correct path.

CHAPTER THREE

Privacy Concerns With Social Media

Have you seen how the adverts on the sites you visit, align neatly with your interests? Believe that is a coincidence? On the web, it simply isn't. Social media apps are notorious for storing and obtaining data about us, and it uses this data to tailor specific ads for us so that we continue using their app and spending on it.

But how does this work?

Information Scraping.

This involves information about individuals being taken from social media, worksites, and online gatherings.

Usually, research organisations are the collectors and they sell this data to businesses or other organisations. Then they isolate and identify unique subtleties in the data. They use these subtleties to manipulate adverts to promote their agenda. You might not realise it, but when you share content online – it can be scraped for this precise kind of data.

One example of genuine online protection infringement occurred in May of 2011. Nielsen Co., a media-research organisation, was discovered scraping each message off PatientsLikeMe's online discussions. Individuals were talking about their issues – in what they believed to be a protected, private space. Many individuals involved felt their web protection was abused.

It has been reported a few times that specific Facebook applications leak personal data about the users who are using them without the users' knowledge!

Here is how the "spillage" works: during the application's download, you are incited to acknowledge specific terms, and once you click "Permit," the application gets an "entrance token." A portion of the Facebook applications releases these entrance tokens to sponsors, allowing them admittance to individual profile information, such as logs and photographs. No disclaimer is displayed declaring that your data is being provided to external entities. Along these lines, your online protection and wellbeing are put in danger.

Examples of applications that have been found to leak distinguishing data include FarmVille and Family Tree.

Online social following.

We, use the "Like", "Retweet", and other catches to send interesting content to our friends. These social gadgets work with "cookies" – these are little records put away on a PC that enable your data to be stored on a particular website. Together, they permit the social sites to remember you on any site that uses these gadgets. Your interests and shopping habits can be followed along these lines.

Other social sites permit organisations to put advertisements, cookies and guides – bits of programming – that can follow you and assemble data about what you are doing on a page. Note: this is broadly used on the web and on sites committed to children and teenagers, which brings up a tremendous concern for their online protection.

How can you keep your information and online conduct from being scraped, leaked, or followed?

- Unfortunately, you can't control the information scraping, but the good news is you can control how much data about yourself you put out. To do so, alter your protection settings right away.

- Even if cookies are not destructive per se, picture them as a calm stalker following all your means. You can erase them from your internet browser and cut-off threats on the PC.

- As for your children's protection, we urge you to stop for a moment to chat with them about online security dangers. Also, use programming to screen their online movement. OpenDNS FamilyShield or Pihole can go about as careful protection monitors on the PC and phone, separately. The Parental Control in the two suites empowers you to see what your children are up to on the web and square their admittance to specific sites or substances.

Tips for securing your social media privacy

For example, platforms such as Facebook, Twitter, Instagram, and Snapchat have become computerised announcements for web clients. Users love sharing their views and news about what's happening in their lives.

Stop and think for a second. This data — some of which is personal — is going up on the web, where it will be immortalised. Outside of your friend and family members, who else is seeing what you post? Spambots, malicious colleagues, and even cybercriminals could take an intrigue. As of late, especially considering the Cambridge Analytica embarrassment, the protection rights on social media sites has been the subject of more extensive public and political discussion.

Given this, we have a few hints to assist you with your protection and keep your informal communication an additional compensating experience.

Review the social media webpage's terms

In the 21st century, data is a significant currency. You wouldn't give out your financial balance data, so why would you part with your security rights? Give specific consideration to what data you are consenting to share when you create a social media account. For instance, as per Facebook's rules, if a user erases any photographs and videos they shared on Facebook, those pictures will be eliminated from the site but could stay on Facebook's servers indefinitely. Also, some content can be erased just if the client for all time erases their record.

Pause for a minute to browse through the legal jargon in the Privacy Policy and Terms of Service before you click "Accept." If it's hard for you to understand the legal-speak, then google it because there are plenty of good explanations online. Some terms may accumulate and sell information identified with what you look at to outsiders for promoting purposes. Make sure your authorisation decisions are directly for you.

Try not to share private data like your complete name and address.

Keep your full name and address to yourself. The same applies for your children. As blameless as it might appear to share individuals' complete names, no one can tell how a stalker or cybercriminal may use that data for their potential benefit. For example, with a blend of your first name and last name, cybercriminals might figure out your email address or buy your email address from the dark web. With this data, they could send you a phishing email that might install malware on your computer and gather information from your gadgets.

Remind young and impressionable people to embrace similar practices, as they might be bound to share individual data. Your children may consider nothing giving their name and address, or other unique subtleties when taking part in an online challenge.

Also, talking about photographs...

Be cautious about posting photographs on social media.

Mull over posting photographs. Regardless of whether you don't expressly post a person's name, you might expose an excessive amount of data in what you thought was a harmless photograph.

Ponder this situation: You want to post pictures of your grandkid in their new sports uniform. What's wrong with this? If the photograph contains the school's name, either on outfits or out of sight, an outsider could find your grandkid's area or school. Consider obscuring or trimming such if not, perhaps that isn't the best photograph to share. Plus, images sometimes contain data that shows where it was taken, with what device, and more. There are ways to get rid of this data from pictures.

Also, shouldn't something be said about that image of your new costly flat-screen TV, or your family room brimming with gifts around the special seasons? Promoting their whereabouts could make your home an enticing target for people who have the wrong intentions.

Web wellbeing 101: hints to keep your children and family protected

The web presents an abundance of data but can also hurt the ones we love. Here are 15 hints to help keep your family protected on the web.

Change social media security settings.

Every social media platform has an area to control security settings. Before you share your post, be aware of who can see, respond, or share.

Cautiously determine whether you need your social media to be visible to everybody, just friends, or also their friends while evaluating your security settings for every platform. You can also make a custom rundown for each post. Tagging friends can be a ton of fun, but also an intrusion of data protection. Also, you might prefer not to be tagged in something. Choose to be notified when another person tags you in a post before it is distributed. Remember, because you may not approve the post on your social media page, it might be published on theirs, openly.

Recognise what kinds of individual information social media platforms store and offer

After signing up to a social media platform, most users give their name, sex, date of birth, and email address. Some social media sites don't stop at that either. You'd be surprised! They gather other data like IP address or the kinds of things you have enjoyed, shared, or commented on. At times, you're given the option to use your Facebook to sign-in to other external websites and applications. While this might be helpful, you could accidentally permit different applications to access your data.

One approach to ensure that you are not oversharing is to browse the fine print. You wouldn't sign a contract without reading it first, so see it as if you are signing a contract. While changing your protection settings on any social media platform, search for the "Applications and Websites" choice under "Settings." Carefully review which sites are using your data.

Consider carefully what individual subtleties you give in your profile.

Social media sites may request extra data when you sign in. You can regularly include your old neighbourhood, schools you've joined, and your current and previous working environment, political affiliations, and general interests. This data can be stored and followed.

As harmless as it might appear, this data could be used to serve you promotions and news things. Many sites may also obtain consent to get to your friend's list, individual interests, and more in their terms of usage.

Know about protection worries in the news, similar to the Cambridge Analytica story

When the Cambridge Analytica outrage stood out as truly newsworthy, individuals noted how delicate their online security is. It's not merely publicists and information firms competing for your precious data; cybercriminals also need admittance to your information or might want to sell it on the dark web.

Keep away from social media webpage posting laments.

It's entirely conceivable that your manager, or the recruitment officer at that organisation you applied to, could check out your social media profile. In case you're posting content that your organisation wouldn't accept — like posts about how much you hate your boss — you should take a step back and reconsider putting your personal info online. When data is out there, it resembles water: it figures out how to run its course toward opportunity. Try not to let what you share today cause issues down the road for you tomorrow.

Address your online security worries with Norton LifeLock

There are different ways to help keep your data hidden on the web. Using a protected VPN is one approach to prevent organisations from following your IP address and viewing your history. Complicated passwords and great digital hygiene go a long way.

If you don't know what a VPN is – it's basically a privacy cloak for your online activity. It conceals your IP address so that nothing can be traced back to you. It's also surprisingly simple to install on your device. *ExpressVPN* is a great one to choose, as is the Norton option detailed below.

You don't have to be a tech nerd to have privacy online.

But if you're not confident, consider introducing Norton Privacy Manager. Or for many layers of insurance on up to 5 gadgets, Norton™ 360 with LifeLock™ includes Norton Secure VPN and parental controls to give you much-needed insight into your children's or grandchildren's online activity history so you can assist them with learning safe web practises. Now you know not to post your complete name and address on the web, isn't that right?

Social Media Privacy Policy Loopholes You Need to Know About

Social media by far is the most impressive asset on the planet for individuals to interact with each other. We will hop in, join and include friends and associations at instant speeds – but how many of us focus on the wellbeing and security of the data we're sharing?

The last time a dialogue box popped up asking you to permit a site or Facebook page to "access your data," did you let it? The best way to share data is to permit them into your space. So, what is sheltered? Do you consider the security approaches to guarantee that your data is secured consistently?

While you may have reviewed each site's protection strategy or built up an essential comprehension of its key components, did you realise that there are escape clauses in these arrangements that put your data and you in danger?

Cybercriminals and the Threat They Pose

Even with just social media alone, you'll notice that there have been various rehashed "Cyber-attacks" against the most prominent social media platforms on the planet in recent years. While they guarantee that no recognisable data about its clients was undermined, it's also hazy whether they'd uncover any information breaches.

Think about this: none of these organisations that detailed being hacked would respond to an inquiry presented to them by the University of Victoria concerning whether they would advise clients if their data had been accessed. doesn't that make you just a little bit suspicious?

Shouldn't something be said about those Privacy Control Settings?

If you're comfortable with the further developed security setting and highlights of these social media sites, you may imagine that your data is secure. But guess what? That is not what those security settings are for! In-network protection highlights permit you to shield your data from being accessed by different clients. They give no additional controls or restrictions regarding outsiders and what the social media organisations themselves may do with your data. Technicalities, aren't they just a pain?

Step-by-step instructions to Protect Your Personal Information

There is a limit to what you can do to secure your data when using social media.

The initial step to securing yourself is to abstain from using recognisable data at any point. You might need to use your complete name to show your profile name; however, if you do,, don't share your first and last name. Instead, use your first and middle name, or find another way around it.

Next, set up an optional email account – separate from the one you share with loved ones. Use this as a spam email account and have this set as your virtual email address inside your profiles. That way, when the social media organisation shares your recognisable data, you won't need to stress over your essential email being immersed with spam mail or cybercriminals!

Third, use a virtual private network (VPN). Your Internet service provider (ISP) is the organisation through which you access the Internet. Your data – including your P.C.'s I.P. address – can be exposed whenever you visit a site. Organisations can use this data to follow where you live, what sites you visit, and other individual data about your personality. With a VPN, it's all under a cloak of invisibility.

By using a VPN to sign on to the Internet, you successfully shroud the data from organisations, hackers, and any other person who's hoping to access it. VPNs usually have a large group of private IP addresses, and when you use the VPN, you will be appointed one of them for the time you're connected. This hides your real I.P. address – and all the data associated with it – from being disclosed to prying eyes.

The enormous amount of data that individuals share on social media – some exceptionally personal – attract different watchers outside family members and friends like moth to a flame. Somebody might even record what you do on your social media for reasons you may not know. The government, spambots, advertisement organisations, malicious colleagues, more awful still, cybercriminals could also have an enthusiasm for your data.

Would you be able to control your security on Social Media?

It's said that every individual is responsible for their social media security. You only need to tick some boxes to move your social media security from "feeble" to "solid" and protect your online data.

Still, controlling your data on social media is not an easy feat. This is because no matter what you do to protect your security on social media, including erasing your record, your friends and family will still share your data. Disposing of your social media applications may not be useful for this situation.

The apparent absence of security on social media makes it imperative to ensure your online protection before sharing anything on any social media platforms.

Step-by-step instructions to Protect Your Privacy on Social Media

Here're a few hints to assist you with ensuring your protection on social media:

1. Read and Understand the Privacy Terms

Each site on the web has security terms, including social media. Before joining any social media platform, it is important that you review and understand their terms of security. Give specific consideration to the protection terms of the data you are enlisting and consenting to share when you join a social media platform. For example, what piece of info can be imparted to the outsider? Can you erase your data from the site forever?

2. Site Features

Guarantee you acquaint yourself with the social media website's usefulness before you broadcast or post any messages. Comprehend who will see your messages, whether it'll be just intended beneficiaries or all clients on the site. Comprehend the protection settings and security weaknesses on the social media website.

3. Alter your Privacy Settings

For each social media site you are using, consistently check the default security settings on their webpage. Most security settings on social media allow sharing your data with other outsider online clients by default. Changing the default security settings may restrict the data they can share.

4. True to life Information

To join most social media platforms, you need to give your data, for example, complete name, year of birth, age, or address. Keep these snippets of data to yourself to restrict what other social media clients think about you. Such data can give cybercriminals enough information. You may tweak the security settings on your media to limit individual data on a similar platform.

5. Record Information

Be very careful and cautious with the details you post on your social media profile. Never share sensitive data, for example, closest schools, political connection, financial balance data, previous or current work environment, Social Security numbers, or general interests, among others. Giving this data may seem harmless, but it may be used to trick you or serve you pointless advertisements.

6. Friends or Contacts

You don't have any commitment to acknowledge a "friend or follow" request of anybody on social media, especially those you don't know. Be cautious while tolerating friends or following friends or contacts with a sharp thought of why you are using the site. Before accepting any follow or friend request research about the individual, (from their timeline) what their identity is, their speciality, and what sort of information they share.

7. Disable Your Location

While modifying your protection settings, always remember to turn off your location. This way, you'll abstain from offering this to organisations you visit.

8. Be cautious about posting photographs on the web

Before you post any photographs, reconsider. Posting photographs on social media has been recognised as one of the unsafe long-range interpersonal communication exercises. For example, a raw, harmless image of your child without a name may uncover an excessive amount of data. Publicising your whereabouts through pictures could make you, your friends and family, or your home an enticing target for cybercriminals or stalkers.

9. Stay away from Clickbait

No social media will assume liability for outsider applications. When provoked to "check which superstar you share a birthday with", abstain from clicking these arbitrary clickbait pages. They are external websites that attempt to catch and abuse your private data.

Security Tips for Privacy on Social Media

Also, with all electronic records, counter the absence of protection on social media by avoiding potential risks to make sure about your security and record data. Here are a couple of security tips:

- Pick a "solid" password, 9 characters or more.

- Use different passwords across all your different social media accounts.

- Abstain from signing into a public P.C. or using friends' phones to sign in to your social media accounts.

- If possible, use a trusted VPN.

- Abstain from using public or shared gadgets to get to your social media accounts.

- Abstain from clicking on social media invites, even the ones sent to you by a friend.

- Secure your gadgets with password insurance to protect your social media and other data if they are taken or lost.

CHAPTER FOUR

Influence Of Social Media On Public Opinion

During the U.S. presidential elections, the media assumed a significant role in driving the competition between the candidates. Social media in particular was a very polarised playing field, with loyal supporters posting content on both ends of the political spectrum.

The broad use of social media in the last decade alone has given researchers a colossal amount of information to investigate the role of social media in influencing real-life events and outcomes. In fact, many organisations are investing their energy and cash to connect on social media and make a lot of information for publicity and ad purposes. They want to focus on clients' input.

Social media and media in general has become our lifeline. It comes in various structures to entertain us and coordinate our joys. There are magazines, papers, web, T.V., news, radio, and social media sites. We're not just exposed to media, we're bombarded by it through innovation, whether our T.V, radios in our car, and advertising. Now, we have the 24-hour news cycle and other streams of information overload on demand.

We can see the impact that social media has when we see hear or see stories about fake news. We're constantly influenced by think pieces, articles and political ideologies disseminated in the media. However, any "news" promoted on social media can potentially be bogus. This influences our opinions on what the acceptable norm looks like (Schneider, Gruman, and Coutts, 2012). An ideal case of this is Jurors in a court case. Twelve people are chosen at random to choose the destiny of a person who may have committed a crime. They are not to address anybody from the media; they must not read the papers or watch the news or examine the case. This is exclusive, to ensure their conclusions are not affected by the media or any other persons.

A study by Schneider et al. (2012) gives an extraordinary case of this when they talk about the perception of drugs in the media during the 1980s. This is called plan setting, implying that the media will affect what we feel is significant in the public arena. As showed by Schneider et al. (2012) "The media didn't affect whether individuals thought the usage of drugs wasn't right, media inclusion brought about individuals believing that the issue was a significant one."

There have been a few attacks on the Canadian military in recent times, and social media immediately held Muslims and the religion of Islam culpable for it. Through the media, ever since 9/11, Muslims have been framed as the blame behind acts of terror. Due to this, incidents of hate crimes against Muslims have risen, along with the anti-muslim sentiment. In a media article distributed by CBC news in Canada, the National Council of Canadian Muslims reviled and denied any association in the attacks and that they too, as Canadians, felt assaulted. They made it clear that Islam in no way promotes acts of terror or violence (CBC News 2012). This is just one great example of media framing and how it influences our biases.

Social Media versus Popular Opinion:

This brings us neatly to the idea that social media has become the new "news" channel.

Twitter and Instagram in particular are slowly becoming the hub for live news in real-time, and people can share comments and have discussions instantly.

In the coming years, it's going to become obvious that social media news will need more regulation beyond simple fact checking – in a crackdown against fake news and polarizing political posts.

How Exposure to Negative Media Influences our Behaviour

Social media broadcasts the news 24-hours every day, 365 days per year. So it's almost impossible to keep away from awful news and the negative impact it has on our lives. Acts of mass violence, fear-mongering assaults and plane accidents, we experience the unremitting surge of savagery from the media every day.

But that's not a bug, it's a feature. By design, our cerebrums zero in on the awful. Much like our fixation on auto collisions and pursuing ambulances, cynicism on social media is hard to overlook, and it can affect how we see our lives and the world. Negative content on social media can prompt negative thoughts, driving us to see our lives as more upsetting than they really may be. Some examination has even shown that awful pictures on the news can cause PTSD-like manifestations. In 2001, the entire world was glued to their T.V. sets when terrorists brought down the Twin Towers in New York City. Studies later showed that pictures of 9/11 set off fear and decreased trust in our country's security. Strangely, the examination also showed that the level of our fear was legitimately connected with the time spent viewing the news.

Experts have also noticed that this introduction to realistic brutality and negative media can either cause an over-refinement, where we become more delicate and cynical or can prompt desensitisation, in which we are numb to things that should offend or upset us.

Sadly, this cynicism can lead us to disregard the numerous things that are positive in the media and on the planet. We just need to look at the posts from loved ones on Facebook, the report about a legend that pulled a young lady from a burning vehicle, or a Tweet about scientists working on cancer research to realise that the personal satisfaction for many individuals has improved.

The Future

There is no uncertainty that social media has made significant commitments to the public this past century. Although still in its outset, social media keeps on taking advantage of the potential for use in the following areas, for example, science, business, amusement, public arrangement and more. Understanding the relationship – both dynamic and intelligent – between social media and society is vital to its further turn of events, and it's positive impact on our lives.

As experts keep on examining the wonder of social media, the ramifications of its influence, how social media affects our translation of data, our turn of events, and our disparities —we will see how to use and create advances to impart, interact, collaborate, talk about, and find new things.

It's all about point of view.

Certainly, for the 'Boomer' generation, social media did not exist until recently and was not part of everyday life. Toys were an extravagance, so going through the day making up games and hanging around outside was typical.

Today, this seems like a totally alien concept to people, especially children.

Which is better?

We should accept that we can't respond to this question. Sure, it was better for our eyes when we weren't investing such a significant amount of energy before screens. Be that as it may, technology has also presented a degree of creativity and opportunity never before acknowledged throughout the entire existence of the world.

What we can examine is the way social media is changing our view of the actual world.

Do we believe the sources giving us the data? What potential is there to become dependent on ever-expanding screen time? We have to rediscover reality in the expressions of Epicurus, the logician: "Moderate to taste the delights of life in plenitude."

Changing Your Perception

Let's get philosophical.

Each dawn is met with nightfall. If that sounds cynical, just remember that each cloud breaks to uncover the daylight. Whichever way the sentiment is expressed, both statements are true. This is true for the two sides of social media – it's optimistic, futuristic hopeful face, and its dark underbelly.

With billions of individuals using social media, the impact one individual can make has never been more significant. That can be both good and bad.

However, one drawback, among many, is that we can quickly become misinformed by fake news or conspiracy theories.

We can appreciate a significant accomplishment of a friend. We can also read a hysterical post proposing that 5G is causing COVID-19 and go out and burn an antenna down for no real reason, ignoring the medical advice to actually stay safe.

Two of a kind

It can't be disregarded that having the option to keep in contact with friends far and wide is an advantage. Truth be told, we can make friends from around the globe without ever being in a similar physical space. This also leaves the potential for us to introduce the inner truth of who we are.

In that lies the oddity of social media. Its qualities can also be its shortcomings. For example, you continually have the option to see your friend's updates. From the outset, this has all the earmarks of being something worth being thankful for. It is. It ought to be.

The test comes when we become jealous of everything our friends seem to be doing. We contrast their online world and our disconnected world, and we regularly feel we don't have the right stuff. We overlook that we just post the splendid spots of our day. So, we wind up contrasting the best of our friend's lives to the most exceedingly terrible of our own.

CHAPTER FIVE

Positive Effects Of Social Media

Whether you believe social media is a force for good or bad, one question we need to ask is this: is social media useful?

According to Hootsuite, 69% of adults from the United States use at least one social media site.

Below is a rundown of the positive and useful effects that are related to social media.

Social media has made it simple to make friends.

Only a couple of years back, it wasn't simple to interact with this many individuals, because the world was smaller.

Now, in our globalised society, we have instant access to millions of potential friends.

The rise in phones' use helped in changing this and helped various individuals interact with each other. After this, the informal communities additionally began appearing, and the whole idea of friendship changed.

Now, it is conceivable to make hundreds to thousands of "friends" over any social media platforms. Sure, they might not be friends spend time within peson, but they are your friends in the virtual world.

Social media helps to cultivate compassion.

Most social media users share details of what's happening in their life, including all the good and bad times, exciting bends in the road and various issues.

When you are sharing your encounters on various sites, you may discover different people who understand you. You may even meet a friend who has just experienced similar trials and can assist you with working through it.

You see that a similar issue has not crushed your friends. This experience will be useful to you.

Social media helps in quick correspondence.

Clearly, your leisure time Is becoming less and less mainly because you oversee both your work and family duties. But you don't have to carve much time out of your busy schedule to text a friend.

Composing a tweet takes just twenty seconds. Writing a text takes less than 10.

Social media causes the world to appear to be little.

Aside from speaking with your loved ones, social media networks help you speak with others in various parts of the world. Communication is now simple. Social media has the intensity of opening up the entire world before you, making it smaller than it used to be.

Regardless of whether your relatives live in other parts of the globe, you can speak with them as though they were living nearby. You can also stay in contact with your friends, with whom you have lost contact. In the realm of social media, physical separation is no longer a significant barrier to maintaining relationships.

Social media helps in building connections.

Social media can assist you in getting back in contact with those you have lost touch with for a while. You can even form a relationship with an individual with whom you share various interests. It may be said that social media is probably the best ground where durable connections can begin. Regardless of whether it is friendship or love, social media will assist you in supporting your relationship.

Social media helps in discovering shared opinions.

Social media sites help in discovering other people who might share similar interests to you, no matter how unique o "nice" those interests may be. There's someone out there for everyone.

But for young people, with the constant reports of cyberbullying in the news – it is important to be careful with strangers online.

It is important for guardians to ingrain solid rules for social media use, including restricting and observing time on the web. Social media doesn't have to be a terrible thing, it's what you make it.

Social Media Can Strengthen Friendships

There is no doubt that friendships are a necessary facet of life. When people have close friendships, they can form their identity in a healthy manner. It is only through associations that we discover who we are as individuals. Friends also keep you grounded, especially during episodes of sadness or poor mental health.

In fact, research has shown that having one healthy friendship can go far in preventing harassment too! Bullies tend to target people without close friends, so having a social network can keep young people protected and insulated against the malice of others.

In a study by Common Sense Media, 52% of adolescents felt that social media improved their kinships, and just 4% felt it hurt them. Also, they found that almost 30% of social media users accept that interpersonal communication causes them to feel surer and more outgoing.

Social Media Is a Vehicle for Doing Good

Regardless of whether young people are creating pledge drives or supporting a significant event, social media can assist them with influencing their networks.

From YouTube videos to Twitter crusades, mobilised young people have more effect on their general surroundings because of social media. Also, their voices are being heard and amplified even more – affording them more political agency.

Social media also brings to light significant issues everywhere in the world, not only those in our immediate networks.

Urge young people to use social media for something other than taking selfies for a more educational experience. Tell them the best way to use it as an apparatus to influence the world. Doing so will enable them to cultivate generosity and appreciation.

▨ Social Media Reduces Feelings of Isolation

While social media can make some adults feel lonelier, analysts are finding the inverse might be the case for younger generations. A study conducted in 2015 found that even though adolescents have fewer friends than they did 10 years back, they report feeling less lonely, and g less segregated.

As adolescents discover themselves, they are navigating a culture that is more individualistic and more outgoing, leading to higher self-esteem.

Through social media, teenagers figure out how to explore interpersonal communication and different strategies for online correspondence – strengthening their communication skills both in real life and online. This improves their skills as communicators in an advanced world.

Social Media Is a Source of Authentic Support

Quite a while back, if young people were keen on an eccentric subject or were wrestling with who they were personally, they would feel minimised and alone. Today, teenagers can interact with others that share similar interests, desires, and concerns. This association causes them to feel validated and secure in what their identity is.

Another way adolescents are discovering support is through online networks. For example, kids battling with issues like chronic drug use and dietary issues can get help and support on the web while never leaving their homes. This is useful for adolescents in little networks or zones where assets might be restricted – so the internet makes help accessible to those who need it.

Young people who have a tendency to be self-destructive can even get quick admittance to quality online help. One case of online help happened when a Reddit Minecraft group worked a high schooler out of self-destruction. Besides posting positive remarks and messages, over 50 clients used voice conferencing to convince the teen not to proceed with it. This is an ideal case of how social media and technology can be beneficial for people.

Social Media Can Build a Platform

Now, there are more opportunities than ever to succeed in a field that does not require years of education. Indeed, social media has made it possible to earn significant money online by building an online presence that can draw in consideration of universities and future managers. Videos, blog entries, photography – whatever the medium, social media has made it possible to monetise hobbies and creative pursuits.

A high schooler who has energy for studying and composing may post book surveys or film videos with their contemplations, thoughts, and remarks. As their work picks up footing on the web, they may even build up a network that could include creators, artistic operators, and distributors.

When this teenager applies for school, they can now reference their social media accounts on school applications. This work exhibits their creativity and development and shows that they are a self-starter.

Building a stage on social media can open plenty of doors for teenagers and assist them with building a positive online presence. It can open them to school grants, school organisations, and even a future vocation. Also, it can change their point of view on social media. It's no longer just a spot to post senseless pictures or watch an advanced show. It turns into an instrument they can use to share their interests and inevitably discover a lifelong way.

Social Media Allows for Personal Expression

Regardless of whether people appreciate singing, composing, or acting, they can post this content online.

A study conducted in 2019 shows that there is an immediate association between self-articulation and self-assurance. When children are being encouraged for being true and consistent with themselves, they become content with what their identity is and are more joyful with their authentic selves.

Conversely, whenever they don't have many chances to communicate, or they don't know individuals with similar interests, they wonder whether the issue is with them.

Social Media Is a Tool for Gathering Information

Social media has become a wellspring of data and news for everyone. From creators and competitors to big names, gourmet specialists, philanthropic associations, and magazines, there is lots to be found in the wild west of the web.

Everyone has access to resources that may come in useful for their friends and loved ones. For example, if they are concerned, a friend may have a dietary problem or chronic drug use, they can assemble data about it. Or then again, if they need to get familiar with a presidential political decision, environmental change, or even find better approaches to eat steadily, they can do that on their social media accounts.

By what means Will Future Well-Being Be Impacted by Technology?

Young people today live in a "consistently associated" world. They use the Internet to do schoolwork, submit papers through Google Docs, Snapchat their friends, tune in to music through Spotify, watch Netflix rather than T.V., and scroll through Instagram. Even their school applications are submitted online.

Since these contraptions, applications, and advances have made their lives easier, more convenient, and more associated, is there such a thing as being excessively computerised? Specialists are isolated on the response. They are not in agreement on what this could mean for the future of the world.

Actually, as per a Pew Research Centre investigation, 33% of specialists expect that computerised life will be harmful overall to teenagers and families in the following decade. Then again, 47% of the specialists surveyed oppose this idea – that it's helpful, not harmful. Also, a few specialists believe there won't be a lot of progress in the coming decade.

Even so, paying little heed to their perspectives, an astounding 92% of the specialists surveyed suggest that governmental approaches and tech organisation practices need to change to decrease the destructive impacts while upgrading the advantages of computerised technology.

A Closer Look at the Study

This non-logical investigation included an analysis of perspectives from almost 1,200 technology specialists, for example, Rob Reich, a teacher at Stanford, Sherry Turkle, the main analyst in human-PC connection, and Ethan Zuckerman, head of the Centre for Civic Media at MIT, among others. This study is important for the Future of the Internet Studies lead by Pew and Elon University's Imagining the Internet Centre.

The initial question the specialists posed was: "Throughout the following decade, in what manner will changes in advanced life sway individuals' general prosperity, truly and intellectually?"

Lee Rainie, head of Internet and Technology Studies at Pew Research, says they attempted the study to measure how industry specialists feel about the developing worries over computerised life and the effect it has on an individual's wellbeing and government assistance.

What they found is that almost everybody they surveyed acknowledged the developing advantages of computerised life. Yet, many are also stressed over the mounting proof that growing usage of technology might prompt issues like distraction, dependence, stress, cyberbullying, and potentially more.

Basic Concerns

By and large, the study revealed some basic subjects among the reactions. For instance, the specialists worried that advanced technology would adversely affect prosperity, predicting that we will see more computerised shortages throughout the following decade.

For example, they envision that individuals' psychological capacities will be tested. What this could mean is that their capacities to think critically, recall data, and focus for significant periods might be debilitated by the instant pace of social media. Generally, they are worried that individuals will battle with mental strength and be less inventive.

Another zone of worry for the respondents is addictions. They caution that a few organisations are planning for their technology to cause dopamine to be secreted.

Dopamine is a substance the body secretes when something is alluring. At its most fundamental level, it is delivered when an individual eats, to remind the body to do it again and again. It is necessary for our survival, but it has been hijacked by the addictive nature of the digital world. Organisations are figuring out how to stimulate these places in the brain, making a longing for adolescents to accomplish something again and again, like playing a specific computer game. Furthermore, industry specialists expect that tech organisations will keep on examining the brain to create innovation that stimulates these pleasurable synthetics in the cerebrum. Doing so will make individuals become "snared" in specific parts of their advanced lives.

Specialists also are worried about the effect advanced life will have on emotional well-being. They are worried that we will see an increase in stress, anxiety, and other mental health issues as our lives get longer and more advanced.

Finally, specialists are worried that as an ever-increasing number of parts of life go computerised, that the dangers to protection and security will increase. There also will be more serious dangers for individual data to be taken. This goes as far as stressing that there will be expanded dangers to majority rule government, public security, and even employment positions. For example, as computerised reasoning and A.I. develops, this may negatively affect the access to jobs, causing a rise in joblessness. For young people entering the workforce in the following decade, this could potentially cause a problem.

Anticipated Benefits

Those who embrace technology and its opportunities will see prosperity, according to the experts.

They additionally foresee individuals will have simpler access to information, data, instruction, and amusement – to even the playing field for everyone in terms of financial gain.

Specialists for Black Dog Institute, a non-profit organisation devoted to developing medicines for psychological sicknesses, concurs that tech could be valuable to future prosperity. For example, they recommend that innovation is changing emotional well-being quicker than anybody expected, and that adolescents are regularly the first to grasp it.

Scientists at Black Dog Institute believe that adolescents are being innovative with their need for emotional wellness care and are using social media, apps and machines to deal with their mental prosperity. This could be amazingly advantageous, taking into account that depression affects 300 million individuals around the globe. Furthermore, the World Health Organisation predicts that by 2030, despondency will have become the single biggest medical services cost at $6 trillion internationally.

Also, with Black Dog's "my compass" program, individuals with mellow anxiety or depression can undoubtedly start looking after their mental health. At this moment, the program has 30,000 dynamic clients. Analysts at Black Dog foresee that advancements like this will continue to develop and positively affect prosperity, particularly for young people who already appear ready to grasp new technologies and advancements.

What Other Studies Say

Various investigations show that innovation is negatively affecting our cerebrums, particularly for younger people. For example, there are various investigations connecting attention deficiency/hyperactivity disorder (ADHD), just as conduct issues, to general technology and social media use.

In one study conducted by the Journal of American Medical Association, teenagers who invest a great deal of energy using social media show an increase in the side effects of ADHD. Understudies who used various kinds of advanced media on different occasions a day were twice as prone to report new manifestations of ADHD as their less carefully dynamic cohorts.

Specialists hypothesise that the momentary satisfaction that young people gain from their computerised gadgets makes it difficult for them to learn motor control, tolerance, and aptitudes that are required for success later on in life.

Then, different investigations have connected informal organisations to changes in psychological wellness too.

For example, Facebook use has been linked to a decline in prosperity. For certain individuals, the more they use social media, the more they become persuaded that their life is dull and exhausting, compared with every other person. This can cause depression and a self-fulfiling prophecy, as the lack of momentum towards change makes it true.

Truth be told, in an investigation directed at the UCLA cerebrum planning focus, they found that specific areas of young minds got stimulated by "likes" on social media, making them crave social media more.

During the investigation, scientists used a fMRI scanner to view the brains of adolescents as they used an invented social media application taking after Instagram. The young adults were shown over 140 pictures where "likes" were accepted to be from their friends. The preferences were allocated by the examination group.

The cerebrum filters uncovered that part of the brain's prize centre, which was particularly active when they saw an enormous number of likes. As showed by analysts, this part of the brain is the same one that reacts when we see pictures of individuals we love or when we win cash.

Analysts state that this prized area of the cerebrum is especially touchy during the teenage years, which could clarify why young people in particular, are attracted to social media.

At long last, there are additional worries that cyberbullying, sexting, and other hurtful practices attached to innovation will develop and affect teens in a negative way. There is now some proof recommending that the effects of bullying can last well into adulthood. Also, cyberbullying and other malpractices are increasing in recurrence and seriousness.

An ongoing report by Pew Research Centre found that most of the teenagers today have encountered cyberbullying at least once. They found that almost 60% of teenagers have encountered some online maltreatment, with verbal abuse and gossip spreading at the top.

Another issue they face is peer pressure, encompassing sexting. Many teenagers are compelled to send such messages when they prefer not to, while others get messages containing indecent photographs without being asked. Not only are there various passionate and legitimate outcomes identified with sexting, it also affects general prosperity that keeps going long after. This can even lead to teens taking risky photos of themselves and posting them online or sending them to people who may not be trustworthy.

Proposed Solutions

The specialists taking an interest in the Pew study offered a few answers for combatting the evil effects of advanced social media use on the future. Beating the rundown of recommendations was the need to build up an "advanced bill of rights". This bill of rights would also include any thought processes to use information gathered to control individuals or make a benefit.

They also proposed something interesting: the promotion of computerised proficiency in schools and creating "push" frameworks that caution guardians and teenagers when their private information is being gathered.

Among young people, the measure of time committed to a few screen exercises has crept up by 42 minutes of the day since 2015, the report said. Almost 62% go through over four hours per day on screen media, and 29% use screens over eight hours every day, as shown by a report by Common Sense Media. This charitable association helps children, guardians, and schools explore media.

Dangers include the potential for youth to be presented with hurtful messages on the web and turn out to be socially disengaged from their friends.

Specialists broke down information from a broadly delegated study of over 1,600 tweens aged 8 to 12 and adolescents aged 13 to 18 about their relationship with media. They followed changes in youth media practices, contrasting current outcomes with those found in the investigation's principal wave in 2015.

The screen media time figures don't mean youth were solely using screen media for that period. Some were using multiple screens across multiple tasks, for example, getting dressed while watching a video, and two hours of scrolling through a phone simultaneously the T.V. was on for two hours would add up to four hours of screen media time by the examination's strategies.

The review analysed young people's usage and happiness during different media exercises. It tended to a wide range of media, remembering reading books, using social media, watching videos, and playing computer games.

A social review is through the rooftop.

There has been an enormous drop in the measure of time tweens, and teenagers spend sitting in front of the T.V. Each generation goes through a 30-minute reduction in T.V. time than four years prior, and each appreciates it less. Watching videos online compensates for the drop, however.

More than twice the same number of young people watch videos consistently than in 2015, and the average time spent viewing has almost multiplied. YouTube rules the online video space, more than streaming services, such as Netflix, Hulu, or Amazon Prime Video.

Even though YouTube says its substance is just for those 13 and above, 76% of tweens state they use the site, and just 23% use YouTube Kids, intended to be a more secure review condition for more youthful individuals.

Among tweens, 53% said YouTube is the site they watch the most, compared with only 7% for YouTube Kids.

Screen use contrasts among socioeconomics.

Here are some interesting statistics that might make you ponder the future of children.

53% of children have their phones by age 11, and almost 70% have one by age 12. Phone ownership among tweens increased from 24% in 2015 to 41% in 2019, and from 67% to 84% among teenagers. Among 8-year-olds, almost 1 in 5 have a phone.

As children get more established, an excess of screen time can meddle with exercises like being genuinely dynamic, doing schoolwork, playing with friends, and investing energy with family. A lot of screen time can cause weight gain, attention issues, sleep disorders, and issues at school.

For children, screen time can include things like exploring a school venture, making music or artistry, or connecting with friends through social media. However, it additionally can consist of less gainful exercises, such as watching inappropriate T.V. shows, visiting dangerous sites, or playing vicious computer games.

A few investigations show that young people go through just about 9 hours every day on the web, on the phone, sitting in front of the T.V., or messing around — so what's a parent to do?

Guardians should keep on setting limits on screen time, preview all shows and games to ensure they're OK, and be mindful of what their children are doing on the web.

CHAPTER SIX

Simple And Effective Ways To Manage Screen Time And Begin Creating Healthier Habits

Young people are progressively OK with the universality of screens in our way of life. Surrounded by individuals on phones, tablets, and P.C., kids are being born into and are growing up with gadget usage when at home, at school, or making the rounds.

Whether or not parents and guardians agree with more screen time for young people, inertly looking through the web and social media has become so inconceivably normal that managing screen time can be an incredible task.

Sorts of Screen Time

Not all screen time is equal. We use hardware for a vast array of purposes, so, the upsides and downsides can fluctuate depending on use.

In a recent report zeroing in on the screen time of tweens and teenagers, Common Sense Media recognised four general classifications to help guardians better comprehend the examples of their family's screen time.

- Passive usage: Watching videos or reading a book are two regular instances of latent use. In their definition, 'uninvolved' isn't intended to be inseparable from 'withdrew.'

- Interactive usage: Playing a computer game or looking through the web is viewed as intuitive computerised usage.

- Communication: Email, text informing, and social media are certain means of communicating in present-day society.

- Content creation: Writing, making music, drawing, coding, and others comprise their special type of screen time.

Guardians can use these overall classifications while taking stock of their family's screen time. For instance, if a kid is a balance of eager coder and Netflix binger, it's useful to perceive the distinction between those screen time uses when choosing the ideal approach to push ahead.

Families should also perceive those various kinds of "content" affect their children. Media that centres on communication and sympathy, for instance, will have an altogether different effect than one that features inappropriate content. Deciding the best content for your children can be as significant as choosing time limits for computerised media usage.

Purposes behind Healthy Limits

With clear inspirations, families will be more effective in reducing their overall screen time. Here are three everyday purposes behind guardians to look for options in contrast to advanced diversion.

Physical Health

One significant advantage of lessening screen time is that it can free a lot of time for physical activity.

The Centres for Disease Control and Prevention suggest that kids and young people get an hour of physical activity every single day. If your kid is selected for a game or other physical activity, meeting this prerequisite on training or occasion days might be straightforward.

However, if your child's exercises are not genuinely demanding, and your school area doesn't organise physical activities, getting to that one-hour mark will require setting aside a few minutes for family practice before or after school.

Hazardous Media Use

Many of us want to check our phones frequently or the strain to react quickly to messages and social media posts. In a recent report entitled *Technology Addiction: Concern, Controversy, and Finding Balance*, 50% of young people detailed that they even felt 'dependent on' their phones. This sentiment of not being able to control media usage can be muddling and upsetting.

Building sound screen time rules in young people's routines as they develop can help them take charge of their media usage further down the road when advanced gadget use turns into a more conspicuous aspect of their everyday exercises.

It's all about building sustainable habits.

Fulfilling Sleep

The ongoing examination has progressively shown that introducing light before sleep time can affect our capacity to fall and remain asleep, particularly for preschool-age kids.

It's not merely the light from phones that can have this impact. Even excessive lights during story-time can smother the production of melatonin, which is the hormone that causes rest typically.

Indeed, looking through social media or sitting in front of the T.V. at sleep time can also keep people up. Short sleep can have a considerable number of negative ramifications for teenagers; inability to think, anxiety, and an improved probability of driving mishaps because of tiredness.

Plans for Healthy Screen Time Limit

Guardians should initially be eager to do their own basic stock screen-time protocol. As young people follow the house rules of their families, guardians should keep steady over their own media usage.

The 5-2-1-0 Rule

The 5-2-1-0 guideline is a necessary arrangement created by the Canadian Childhood Obesity Foundation to assist families with remaining sound.

It prescribes families cling to the four observing guidelines:

- Five or more servings of vegetables.
- Two hours or fewer of screen time.
- One hour of physical activity.
- Zero sugary drinks.

In the beginning, guardians may need to depend on a clock for screen time limits. But since it's straightforward, this arrangement is actualised by families with offspring, everything being equal.

Sleep Hygiene

Controlling screen time use before sleep time is only one aspect of this, which can also cover different practices, such as daytime naps, caffeine ingestion, exercise, and diet.

With screen time, limit computerised gadget use in the last 2 hours before bed is best. If screen time has become an aspect of your family's sleep schedule, it might help push ahead with a 'no longer of any concern' attitude. That implies no screens in rooms and moving charging stations into the living room or kitchen.

Give Alternatives

Something as straightforward as having little everyday errands can keep a child's screen time at a sound level. Guardians can also typically merge family-holding time into their after-school and end of the week plans. Playing tabletop games, going for nature strolls, or baking a little treat are, on the whole, simple ways families can decrease computerised media usage together. They also foster a stronger bond with teens.

Strategies to Limit Your Teen's Screen Time

Without grown-up supervision, most young teens would spend practically the entire day behind a screen. Regardless of whether they're messaging on their phones or watching videos on their P.C., their hardware use might be out of control. If your kid says, "everybody is doing it", they might be right. However, that doesn't mean there aren't any side effects. How about we look at procedures you can use to restrict your teen's screen time and how it can profit your entire family?

A lot of Screen Time for Teens Is the Norm.

A recent report by the Kaiser Family Foundation found that 8-to 18-year-old kids dedicate seven hours and 38 minutes to amusement media every day.

The total time might be compared to over 53 hours every week or 2770 hours every year.

When the investigation represented the young people performing various tasks endeavours, they found that adolescents are presented to around 10 hours and 45 minutes' worth of media content every day.

Outcomes of Excessive Screen Time

An excessive amount of screen time has been connected to a host of issues. Unnecessary electronic use can increase the risk of obesity, meddles with social exercises and family time, and negatively affects a high schooler's psychological wellbeing.

Interestingly, a study conducted in JAMA Paediatrics found that parental checking of a teen's media can have defensive advantages on their school, social, and physical results. Setting aside the effort to plan the best method is hugely worth your time (and the opposition you will get) as a parent.

Realising that guardians can have any kind of effect on their kid by restricting screen use, what would you be able to do? What procedures have helped different guardians execute and implement these standards?

Every child or teen is unique, and one technique may work for one kid over another. We trust that just a few of these ten procedures will assist you in setting good cut-off points for your child in any event.

Make Screen Time a Privilege

One way screen time has changed lately is that it's regularly felt to be a privilege rather than a benefit. If you grew up viewing the only four channels available, you might have felt blessed to watch an animation on Saturday morning. The mix of having pretty much anything accessible on a screen adds more weight on guardians to state when a child or teen can and can't have screen time.

Clarify that screen time is a benefit that should be earned. From the outset, this might be troublesome. The exercises from figuring out how to defer the delight of screen time and control their motivations will remain with your kid for quite a while.

Also, clarify that the benefit of screen time can be revoked at any point. Tell your child to do schoolwork and errands first before rewarding themselves with the T.V. or the P.C.

Instructions to Model Appropriate Screen Time

Demoralise Multitasking

Most young people believe they're great at performing various tasks. They attempt instant messaging while getting their work done or using social media while chatting on the phone. If your child has a phone, you're likely exceptionally acquainted with them doing such.

Discourage your child or teen from doing two things at once and talk about how performing various tasks meddles with their focus and attention. Multi-tasking isn't real, it usually involves doing more than one task at a low-quality level.

Build up Clear Rules about Electronics

Most young people, particularly adolescents, aren't grown enough to deal with free rules with their hardware. Establishing clear rules keeps your teenager safe and helps your high schooler use sound judgment with computer games, phones, T.V., and P.C.

Instances of useful guidelines include making some set memories when screens should be off around evening time and eliminating screens from rooms.

Thoughts for Non-Screen Activities

A few things a child or teen can do as opposed to looking at a screen include:

- Communicating with guardians and kin
- Socialising with friends
- Reading stimulating books
- Being inventive and using their creative mind
- Playing outside and appreciating nature
- Doing schoolwork
- Carrying out family tasks

- Getting enough rest

Think of a portion of the exercises you appreciated growing up and how it would be distinctive and cool today. Try not to let your kid pass up those chances!

Guardians Need to Work Together

Restricting screen time is fine if guardians cooperate. Inter-parent struggle (strife between guardians) setting these cut-off points is related to a kid having more clashes in their connections.

Before setting media limits with your child,, ensure you cooperate with your partner to introduce these standards as a unified group. For guardians who aren't together, this can be more troublesome. If you are facing this, attempt to see that joining (regardless of whether separated or isolated) is significant for your kid's strength.

If this remaining part is an issue, it may be useful to involve an outsider, for example, a specialist, to look at manners by which you can bargain so your child has their screen time restricted without making it a zone of conflict between guardians.

The Bottom Line

Surely, extreme screen time can harm our kids academically and from both a physical and mental outlook. Simultaneously, screen time is making our children docile in the face of the many exercises which are significant in supporting the family and kinships.

Try to implement some of the measures outlined here to decrease your child's screen time. If you need something positive to balance the opposition you will get from your child, monitor the exercises which supplant screen time. You might be amazed. Gadgets and screens aren't disappearing any time soon, and there are positive perspectives to their usage as well.

As guardians, we can show our kids to use these screens as an advantage, which is beneficial.

CHAPTER SEVEN

Simple And Effective Ways To Manage Screen Time And Begin Creating Healthier Habits For Adults

Everyone has a phone in their pockets, iPads on bedside tables, P.C. at school and work, and an all-you-can-eat selection of top-quality T.V. and films are accessible at whatever point and any place we need it. With such an appetising digital menu, it's no big surprise that the time children and guardians spend on screens is increasing.

Even though we realise that an excess of screen time is bad for our psychological, physical, and emotional well-being, most families today battle to keep screen time under control.

Here are ten different ways you can enable your family to oversee screen time:

1. Make a family media plan

It's the guardians' obligation as far as kids are concerned; however, children will have a simpler time tolerating those cut-off points if they feel they've been engaged with the dynamic. Call a family meeting to share your interests about screen time and request your children's help to make a family media plan that will become part of the house rules. One device that may help is the social media time adding machine made by the American Academy of Paediatrics, which makes a visual breakdown of how much time your family spends on screens compared to other daily needs.

2. Be available when screens are used

Small kids get more out of instructive programming when grown-ups converse with them about what's going on, on-screen. For more grown-up kids, games, T.V., and films can start significant conversations about family values, life wisdom, or open doors for family bonding. Being available when your kids are on screens helps safeguard them too, as you can intercede if you notice that what they're doing or watching isn't age-appropriate.

3. Talk with your children about worthy screen use

Similarly, as we show our children how to go across neighbourhood roads securely, cycle on the right half of the street, and what to do whenever called by a stranger on the play area; we have to show our children how to remain safe on the web and how to ensure screen time isn't affecting sleep, dinner time, recess, or associating with loved ones.

4. Encourage screen use that is instructive, dynamic, or social

Screen time isn't all terrible! Urge children to use their gadgets to FaceTime faraway relatives, make home films or movements, and become familiar with things that intrigue them, including exercise, artwork, or activities.

5. Help your kids pick great substance

For small kids, search for programmes that aren't too relentless or vigorous, with characters, storylines, or subjects that mirror your family's qualities. A decent source to help assess whether a show or game is proper for your kid is Common Sense Media. This site gives family-friendly evaluations to movies, T.V. shows, and games just as age suggestions and data about sensitive subjects like sex, brutality, language, and dubious subjects.

6. Timetable "sans screen" times

One little change that can help keep screens under control is to mark when screens are not allowed for specific periods (Mom and Dad as well!). You may conclude that screens are not permitted during playdates, for instance, or in specific spots, like the family room. A few families limit screen use either to after school or ends of the week, contingent upon their timetable. Others leave gadgets at home while on an extended get-away or announce Sundays as "sans screen". There's no set in a stone manner to do this, yet it helps everybody remain on target to be clear about when your family is "sans screen".

7. Mood killer screens when not being used

Screens are amazing attention magnets and can occupy kids from dynamic or inventive play. You can enable your children to remain focused on different exercises by turning screens off when not being used. Don't let boredom or tantrums make you take the easy way out!

8. Turn screens off at any rate one hour before bed

Light from screens can lead a few children to have trouble nodding off. Turning screens off well before sleep time helps ensure kids go to bed on schedule and wake up feeling rested.

9. Cut-off screen use

Giving over your phone or tablet is frequently a method to keep kids calm at cafés or during long buggy strolls, yet it's ideal to spare this if all else fails! Take a stab at pressing a "bustling pack" with little toys, coloured pencils, paper, little pots of play dough, or different things to give small kids something to do. You can also have a go at playing basic games like I Spy or let babies out of the buggy to walk or creep around for a piece if they get fastidious.

10. Put screens beyond reach during dinner time

Family mealtimes are to interact with one another, and for children to learn dinner time decorum and practice conversational abilities. When screens are at the table, not only would it be able to impede these associations, it can also make kids less mindful of when they are full, which could lead them to overeat. For adults, dinnertime is a significant opportunity to turn off digital media. Most messages and social media pings can sit tight for your answer until dinner is finished!

Quit crapping with your phone (yes, we mean you!)

For most of humanity, one thing we definitely have not needed is a bathroom buddy (for the able-bodied at least). Taking your phone with you to go number two isn't just gross; it's additionally a weak reason to invest more energy checking scores, swiping through social media, or messing around. The pressure on your body while you endlessly scroll is also bad for your digestive organs.

Order your (and your friends') Googling propensities

My friends genuinely disdain me for this yet love me for it (I think). Whenever you're discussing a tidbit over dinner with friends, stop yourself and every other person from getting a phone to google it.

If you never discover what the state fledgeling of Nebraska is, what difference does it make? In return, the enthusiastic discussion proceeds and isn't stopped by a conclusive truth.

Quit taking so many photographs

Much the same as over-googling keeps your cerebrum from holding data; photograph taking keeps your mind from framing actual memories. In three studies, individuals who didn't take photographs during an encounter had more accurate recollections than the others.

If that is not enough motivation to leave your phone in your pocket, *then I don't have the foggiest idea.*

Abandon your phone

Okay, this sounds dramatic, but hear me out. At the ends of the week, I take quite a while - now and then hours - to react to messages. That is because my phone is seldom with me. At lunch or on a stroll, I abandon my phone and invest more energy "living in the moment" and away from my screen.

Try not to use your phone as your morning timer.

Brief, you're getting the morning's alert, and the following 30 minutes, you're in different applications. Keeping your phone outside the room reduces screen time. However, it may also decrease some anxiety. An ongoing study found that the individuals who rested close to their phones were twice as liable to report nomophobia.

Use a smartwatch or tracker

My greatest phone habit challenge was what I call the "bunny opening." I would get a warning - even only an instant message - and abruptly, I'm in the rabbit hole, checking different applications and spending many minutes on my phone.

But, by using a smartwatch or wellness tracker with warning highlights, you can check the time and get important messages without falling into the rabbit hole.

The significant indicator here is that smartwatch warnings can undoubtedly turn crazy, so you'll be focused on topping the notices you get on your wrist.

Tell your loved ones.

Similarly, telling your friend and family, you're reducing screen time will keep you accountable with any aim.

Mood killer, The Unnecessary App Notifications

If you turn off pointless notifications, you probably won't check your phone as much. It's that simple.

You're probably getting an entire heap of message pop-ups that you never click on, for apps whose function in your life requires no criticalness. For instance, you may get message pop-ups for applications you haven't signed on to in some time, which are trying to say some variant of "We miss you!"

Let's say you need to stop your application notifications, change how regularly you get particular notices, or change the sort of notification you get (like a standard versus a genuine caution). In that case, you can go to "Notifications," found in your Settings application. From that point, you can see the settings you have for your app.

Author's Conclusion

BREAKING FREE FROM THE SHACKLES

Let's not get the wrong idea, social media is, and will continue to be, one of the most powerful tools of our time and it's here to stay. Yet, it can be harmful if we allow it to be. Hopefully, this book has provided some useful tips and insight into how to manage usage and watch out for the early warning signs of social media addiction.

The power it has over people if unchecked can be extremely dangerous; family members can get stuck in echo chambers of hate, children can miss out on early developmental lessons and much more. Everyone should be made aware of the effects because if not addressed, or taken care of, social media could cause national and international problems in the long run.

Social media stunts interpersonal growth and increases narcissism in many internet users, and even if the user is not psychologically affected by social media, they are still in danger.

Nobody is immune to the harmful side effects of social media which also include identity theft, stalkers, or hackers. Social networking allows hoaxes and false information to cause widespread chaos. For this reason, I do worry about what the future has in store for us and the youth of today who spend so much time in this virtual world.

If you take one thing away from this book, let it be this: it's your time and data you are giving away to these corporate companies, would you provide this amount of data and time for anything else in the same unquestionable manner?

Looks like it's time to release those shackles.

References

1. Anderson M, Jiang J. Teens, social media & technology 2018. Pew Research Centre. 2018; 31:2018.

2. Kelly Y, Zilanawala A, Booker C, Sacker A. Social media use and adolescent mental health: Findings from the UK Millennium Cohort Study. EClinicalMedicine. 2018; 6:59-68.

3. Smith A, Anderson M. Social Media Use in 2018 [Internet]. Pew Research Centre Internet. Science & Tech. 2018.

4. Salomon I, Brown CS. The selfie generation: examining the relationship between social media use and early adolescent body image. The Journal of Early Adolescence. 2019; 39(4):539-60.

5. Weinstein E. Influences of Social Media Use on Adolescent Psychosocial Well-Being:'OMG'or 'NBD'? (Doctoral dissertation). 2017.

6. Michikyan M, Suárez-Orozco C. Adolescent media and social media use: Implications for development. Journal of Adolescent Research. 2016; 31(4):411-414.

7. Keles B, McCrae N, Grealish A. A systematic review: the influence of social media on depression, anxiety and psychological distress in adolescents. International Journal of Adolescence and Youth. 2020; 25(1):79-93.

8. U.S. Department of Health & Human Services. Common Mental Health Disorders in Adolescence. Hhs.gov. https://www.hhs.gov/ash/oah/adolescent-development/mental-health/adolescent-mental-health-basics/common-disorders/index.html. Updated May 2019.

9. National Institute of Mental Health. Mental Illness. Nimh.nih.gov. https://www.nimh.nih.gov/health/statistics/mental-illness.shtml. Updated February 2019.

10. Twenge JM, Joiner TE, Rogers ML, Martin GN. Increases in depressive symptoms, suicide-related outcomes, and suicide rates among US adolescents after 2010 and links to increased new media screen time. Clinical Psychological Science. 2018; 6(1):3-17.

11. Kelly Y, Zilanawala A, Booker C, Sacker A. Social media use and adolescent mental health: Findings from the UK Millennium Cohort Study. EClinicalMedicine. 2018; 6:59-68.

12. Allcott, H., Braghieri, L., Eichmeyer, S., & Gentzkow, M. The welfare effects of social media. American Economic Review, 2020; 110(3), 629-76.

13. Woods HC, Scott H. # Sleepyteens: Social media use in adolescence is associated with poor sleep quality, anxiety, depression and low self-esteem. Journal of Adolescence. 2016; 51:41-9.

14. Scott H, Biello SM, Woods HC. Identifying drivers for bedtime social media use despite sleep costs: the adolescent perspective. Sleep Health. 2019; 5(6):539-45.

15. Barry CT, Sidoti CL, Briggs SM, Reiter SR, Lindsey RA. Adolescent social media use and mental health from adolescent and parent perspectives. Journal of Adolescence. 2017; 61:1-1.

16. Holland G, Tiggemann M. A systematic review of the impact of the use of social networking sites on body image and disordered eating outcomes. Body Image. 2016; 17:100-10.

17. Fardouly J, Vartanian LR. Social media and body image concerns: Current research and future directions. Current Opinion in Psychology. 2016; 9:1-5.

18. Selkie EM, Fales JL, Moreno MA. Cyberbullying prevalence among US middle and high school-aged adolescents: A systematic review and quality assessment. Journal of Adolescent Health. 2016; 58(2):125-33.

19. Kuehn KS, Wagner A, Velloza J. Estimating the magnitude of the relation between bullying, e-bullying, and suicidal behaviours among United States youth, 2015. Crisis: The Journal

of Crisis Intervention and Suicide Prevention. 2018.

20. Ottawa shooting: Canadian Muslims denounce attacks. (2014, October 23). Retrieved from CBC News Ottawa: http://www.cbc.ca/news/canada/ottawa/ottawa-shooting-canadian-muslims-denounce-attacks-1.2810489

21. Schneider, F. W., Gruman, J. A., & Coutts, L. M. (2012). Applied Social Psychology. Thousand Oaks: Sage Publications, INC.